THE ANIMALS' CHRISTMAS
AND OTHER STORIES

At last, the baby gave a cry and the animals drew
near the rough crib in which he lay. Then, as the
baby opened his eyes, the animals sank to their
knees.

'This,' said the cow, 'is no ordinary baby.'

Everyone was silent, even the ox. But after a
while, the peace was broken by a loud banging.
The door burst open and in walked three
shepherds, followed by their sheep.

'Well really!' exclaimed the ox. 'Without a "by
your leave" or a "would you mind?" Some people
have no manners!'

AVRIL ROWLANDS worked for the BBC for
many years and has written screenplays for
children's television as well as books. In between
writing she also runs training courses in television
production. Her hobbies include swimming,
walking, theatre and steam railways.

With especial thanks to my very dear friends
Leslie Guest and Maureen Beattie
who inspired so many of the stories

The Animals' Christmas

and other stories

Avril Rowlands
Illustrations by Rosslyn Moran

LION
Children's Books

Text copyright © 1997 Avril Rowlands
Illustrations copyright © 1997 Rosslyn Moran
This edition copyright © 1997 Lion Publishing

The author asserts the moral right
to be identified as the author of this work

Published by
Lion Publishing plc
Sandy Lane West, Oxford, England
www.lion-publishing.co.uk
ISBN 0 7459 3699 7

First edition 1997
10 9 8 7 6

A catalogue record for this book is available
from the British Library

Printed and bound in Great Britain
by Cox & Wyman Ltd, Reading

CONTENTS

TO BEGIN...

There is a legend that on the first Christmas night animals knelt beside the crib at Bethlehem to worship the newborn king. Perhaps they understood more than many people at that time, and perhaps there are things that animals can show us now about Christmas past and present...

1

THE CROW GETS TIED UP

It was cold in the garden and the small grey squirrel shivered as she nibbled a nut. 'It's not very warm, is it?'

'What do you expect in December?' said the large black crow, who was strutting up and down the garden fence.

'I wish I h-had a th-thick fur coat,' said the mouse, whose teeth were chattering with cold.

'If you had wings like me, you could fly around and keep yourself warm,' said the crow, flapping his wings up and down.

A worm popped his head up, out of the ground. 'Frost this morning,' he said in a worried voice. 'Ground's hard. Gave me quite a headache trying to break the surface.'

'I *could* give you a bigger headache,' said the crow, eyeing him with interest. 'Luckily for you, I'm not hungry right now.'

'Not hungry!' the mouse repeated, amazed. 'I'm always h-hungry. I do h-hate this t-time of the year. No f-food, no water, f-freezing cold.'

'You can have one of my nuts, if you like,' offered the squirrel.

The old dog, who was lying on the patio in a patch of winter sun, stretched herself.

'Never mind,' she yawned. 'It'll soon be Christmas.'

'What's C-Christmas?' asked the mouse.

The old dog looked surprised. 'Don't you know? I thought everyone knew.'

'*I* know!' exclaimed the crow, boastfully.

'What is it then?' asked the squirrel.

'It's um... it's... well, if you don't know what Christmas is, I don't see why *I* should tell you,' the crow replied.

'I don't think you know at all,' said the squirrel.

The old dog thumped her tail. 'It's when Jesus was born.'

'Who's Jesus?' asked the mouse.

'A very special human,' the dog explained.

'Humans can't be special,' said the crow. 'They can't fly!'

'Neither can I,' said the squirrel.

'Nor me,' the worm added, rather wistfully.

'Humans *can* fly,' said the dog. 'They fly in great machines.'

'Anyone can fly in a *machine*,' scoffed the crow. 'There's nothing clever about flying in a *machine*. It's not like having your own wings and feathers now, is it?'

'Tell us about this Jesus,' the worm asked, eagerly.

'Well, he was born in a stable around this time of the year,' the dog began.

'Why wasn't he born in a hospital?' the mouse demanded.

'I don't know.' The dog frowned. 'I don't think they had hospitals then. It all happened in a far-off country a long, long time ago. Two thousand years ago.'

'So what's it got to do with us now?' demanded the crow, quite forgetting that he had said he knew all about it.

'Every year humans celebrate his birthday, because Jesus is the son of our Maker.'

'Yes, but it's only important for *humans*,' said the crow. 'Not for *birds*—otherwise, why wasn't Jesus born a crow?'

The dog shook her head. 'I don't know.'

'Or why wasn't he born a mouse?' asked the mouse.

'Or a squirrel,' added the squirrel.

'Or even a worm,' whispered the worm.

The crow rounded on him. 'Who would ever want

to be born a *worm*?' he sneered.

The worm dived down into the soil.

'So what's so special about this Jesus?' the crow demanded.

'I told you,' said the dog. 'He is the son of our Maker, and he was born as a human baby.'

'He should have been born a crow,' said the crow. 'We're much cleverer than humans. *And* we can fly!'

'I wish you'd shut up about flying,' said the mouse.

'Hush,' said the squirrel. 'Someone's coming.'

Everyone fell silent as a man and a woman came out of the house. One of them carried a long string of

bright lights, the other carried a stepladder. They went over to a tall fir-tree and placed the ladder beside it.

'It's grown quite a bit since last year,' said the woman.

'Yes, it has,' the man agreed. He climbed up the ladder, carrying the string of lights, but he was unable to place them on the very top of the tree.

'What are they doing?' asked the worm, poking his head out of the soil. 'I can't see.'

'They're trying to put a string of lights on the top of the tree,' said the crow. 'But they're not tall enough. Even on a ladder.' He flew off the fence and circled the tree. 'S'easy if you're a bird,' he boasted. 'I told you humans weren't as clever as us.'

'I don't think being able to fly is clever at all,' the mouse said. 'It's just that you're born with wings, like I'm born with a tail. Cleverness doesn't come into it!'

The man and the woman disappeared into the garage and came out with a long pole. They hooked the string of lights to one end, and then the man climbed back up the ladder and once again tried to place the lights on top of the tree.

Everyone watched with interest.

'No chance,' scoffed the crow. 'That pole's not long enough.'

'What they need is one of those machines you were on about,' said the squirrel. 'It could fly over the

13

tree and drop the lights on to it.'

'What they need,' said the crow, 'is a crow. I could do it easy as anything!'

The worm wriggled. 'What I don't understand is why they're trying to put lights on the tree in the first place,' he said.

'Because,' said the dog, 'it's Christmas.'

'Oh let's leave it for now and go and get warm,' said the woman. 'My hands are frozen.' She turned to the dog. 'Din-dins?'

The dog got up and shook herself lazily. 'I'm off. There's a nice fire inside and my food'll be waiting.'

'Lucky for some!' said the crow.

'Wait a minute,' said the mouse. 'So Christmas is about Jesus' birthday then, is that it?'

'Well, yes,' said the dog. 'And no.'

The crow laughed. 'That's a *really* helpful answer, I don't think.'

The dog thought for a moment. 'There isn't just one answer,' she said at last. 'It's about being kind, and... and helping others...' She stopped and thought some more. 'It's about a whole lot of things,' she finished, and trotted into the house.

'"*Din-dins*",' mimicked the crow scornfully. 'I ask you!'

'I wish *I* had a nice fire and food waiting,' said the mouse, enviously.

14

It began to get dark and a cold wind began to blow. The squirrel ran along the fence to find her store of nuts and the worm disappeared into his hole in the ground.

'They're not going to get those lights on that tree today,' said the mouse.

The worm popped out his head. 'Wouldn't it give them a nice surprise if they found *we'd* done it?'

The crow looked him up and down. 'You! You haven't even got any legs, let alone wings—so I don't know how you'd get up that tree!'

'No need to be personal,' said the worm.

'Of course, it'd be easy for *me* to do it,' the crow said.

'So why don't you, instead of just boasting?' said the mouse, crossly.

The crow opened his beak to say no, then changed his mind.

'All right, then. I will.'

He swooped down from the fence, picked up the end of the string of lights in his beak, and flew up to the top of the tree. But, just as he was about to drop the lights on to the top-most branch, there was a gust of wind, and the lights wrapped themselves tightly round and round the crow's body. Unable to fly, the crow fell straight into the top of the fir-tree.

'Ouch! Ow!' yelled the crow, as the pine needles stuck into his feathers.

'Serves you right!' called the mouse.

'Don't just sit there—do something!' the crow called back, crossly.

'Sorry,' said the worm. 'I can't climb.'

'And I haven't a head for heights,' said the mouse. 'They make me go all dizzy.'

'Fine lot of friends you are,' snapped the crow. 'And I only wanted to give the people a nice surprise—because it's Christmas.'

'No you didn't,' retorted the mouse. 'You wanted to show off, because you can fly!'

The squirrel ran back along the fence, nibbling a nut. 'What's all the row about?' she asked.

'The crow's got stuck in the top of the tree and none of us can help him,' the mouse explained.

The squirrel looked up at the tree. It was very tall. She called to the crow. 'Just stay right where you are!'

'Is that meant to be a joke?' shouted the crow, crossly.

'I only meant that if you try to move you might fall—and it's a long way to the bottom,' replied the squirrel. She took a deep breath and scampered right up to the top of the tree while the animals watched. Catching the string in her paws, she ran round and round the crow, unwinding the lights until they fell into the branches.

'There,' she said. 'You're free now.'

The crow flew off, flapping his wings, and the squirrel made her way wearily to the ground. As she reached the bottom, the man and the woman came out of the house.

'Where have the lights gone?' asked the man. 'Has someone stolen them?'

They both looked round, and then the woman pointed. 'Look! They're right at the top of the tree!'

'However did they get there?'

'I don't know. Someone must have put them up for us.'

'Well, whoever it was, I'm very grateful,' said the man.

That evening, the dog, the squirrel, the crow, the worm and the mouse gathered round the tree, which glowed with hundreds of tiny different twinkling lights.

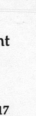

'I did that,' said the crow, proudly. 'That was *me* did that!'

'You'd never have done it if *I* hadn't suggested it,' said the worm.

'And you only did it to show off,' said the mouse. 'Not to be kind and helpful. It was the squirrel who *really* put the lights up there,' he added. He turned to the squirrel. 'Didn't you?'

But the squirrel did not answer. Tired out from her hard work, she had fallen fast asleep.

2

THE DONKEY MAKES A CHOICE

Two donkeys plodded along a dusty road towards town. They walked slowly and wearily, with heavily-laden baskets strapped to their sides.

'My panniers are heavier than usual,' grumbled Ezra. 'And they're not evenly filled.'

Moses said nothing. His panniers, too, seemed heavier than usual, but he did not complain for he was a patient, uncomplaining donkey.

'You'd think, wouldn't you, that they could have filled the panniers evenly,' Ezra went on grumbling. 'I'm not sure I can walk all the way to town with one side heavier than the other!'

Moses sighed. 'You know, Ezra, you must be the worst-tempered donkey in the whole of Nazareth.'

'So tell me why I should be anything else?'

'Perhaps you're the worst-tempered in the whole of Israel,' Moses amended.

Ezra snorted. 'Here we are, carrying these great, heavy panniers—no, these great, heavy, *uneven* panniers—to town, when we could be lazing in a field, eating clover and sweet grass, running and kicking up our heels—and you complain that I'm bad-tempered. What do you expect?'

'Oh, life's not so bad,' said Moses.

'Isn't it? Beasts of burden, that's all we are,' Ezra grumbled, flicking his tail. 'It's not as if we ever get any thanks for what we do—just kicks and lashes if we don't work hard enough.'

'It could be worse,' said Moses. 'Look at Nathan. His master beats him all the time.'

'I've no sympathy,' said Ezra. 'If it was me, I'd run away.'

Moses glanced at him. 'Why don't you, then?' he asked. 'Why do you stay?'

Ezra looked at the master's son, who was walking beside the two donkeys, a large stick in his hand.

'Fat chance,' he said.

They went on in silence.

Suddenly Moses stopped. A child was sitting at the side of the road. His fists were crumpled into his eyes and his cheeks were stained with tears. His clothes were torn and dusty.

'Just look at that,' Moses said. 'Poor little scrap.'

Ezra glanced at the child. 'What's poor about

him?' he asked. 'He's got clothes, hasn't he? That's more than we've got. And I expect he gets more to eat than we do. Besides, I hate humans who snivel. You'd never catch me crying—and my life's a lot harder than his.'

The master's son went over to the child and spoke to him. Then he picked him up and sat him on Moses' back. The child stopped crying and began to stroke Moses' soft grey ears as the donkey moved off.

'Glad he didn't try putting that child on *my* back,' said Ezra. 'I'd have soon had him off!'

'Oh I don't mind,' said Moses stoutly, but after a bit he began to walk more slowly, burdened by the extra weight.

'You'll be tired out by the time we get back—and it serves you right,' Ezra said, with a sidelong glance at Moses. He shivered suddenly. 'It's going to be a cold night. I'd give a lot for a nice warm blanket and a big bowl of oats. But will we get it? No chance. Especially with us coming in late because you chose to give that snivelling child a lift into town.'

'I didn't *choose* to give him a lift into town, but I'm quite happy to do it,' said Moses. 'I hate to see children crying.'

'Soft, that's what you are,' said Ezra. 'He was probably doing it deliberately. You're a fool, Moses!'

'Well, I'd rather be a happy fool than a miserable

old stick like you,' said Moses.

Ezra snorted in disgust and they finished their walk into Nazareth in silence.

Now, unknown to the two donkeys, the Emperor Augustus, who lived a long way away, had just told everyone to register in the place where they were born, in order to be counted. He wanted to know how many people lived in the Roman Empire. This meant an enormous upheaval.

'This registration's good news for us, though,' Ezra's master said to his wife. 'We don't have to travel anywhere because we were born here. But others do, and people will pay a lot to hire horses, carts, mules and donkeys.' He rubbed his hands. 'If we wait for a day or two, we should get an excellent price.'

'We might get a good price for hiring out Moses,' his wife said. 'But what about Ezra? We'd never get him to carry anyone.'

'I'd sell that good-for-nothing donkey tomorrow, if only someone would buy him,' said Ezra's master. 'But I don't suppose anyone would.'

Soon, every donkey and horse, every mule and ox, every cart and chariot in Nazareth had been hired out to those who had to travel far away in order to register. Moses was eventually hired, for a fat fee, to a couple who were going to Jericho.

Moses was pleased.

'I've never been anywhere as far,' he confided to Ezra. 'It'll be an experience.'

'It'll be an experience all right,' Ezra said, unimpressed. 'An exhausting experience. Have you seen the size of them? Large isn't the word! And the amount of luggage! Anyone would think they're moving house, instead of just going to register.'

'Well, I'm looking forward to it,' said Moses. 'I think every donkey ought to travel at some point in his life. It'll broaden my horizons. I hope you're hired for a nice trip, Ezra.'

'Me? Huh! Anyone tries to hire me and I'll bite their hands!'

And that is just what Ezra did. When anyone enquired about hiring him, he bit, not only their hands but any part of them he could reach, or he kicked them, or he threw them off his back. Soon, he was the only donkey left in Nazareth. This made him feel lonely, as he had no one to hear his grumbles, and he had to work harder than ever, to make up for the loss of Moses. So he grew more and more bad-tempered.

One evening, he reached his stable to find his master waiting with a man and a young girl.

His master was shaking his head. 'Of course I'd like you to hire him,' he said. 'But it's only fair to tell you that that donkey's the last one left in town and you know why? Because he's vicious. He kicks, he bites, and he's thrown everyone who's tried to mount him. He's an evil and bad-tempered beast.'

'We've tried everywhere else,' said the man, whose name was Joseph. 'And I must hire something. Mary's expecting a baby and she can't walk all the way to Bethlehem.'

'Well, it's up to you,' said Ezra's master. 'But I wouldn't chance it myself.'

Joseph turned to Mary. 'What do you think?'

Mary gave Ezra a long look which made him feel uncomfortable, so he turned his back on her.

'I think,' she said quietly, 'that we should talk to the donkey and ask if he'll carry me.' She smiled. 'It's no small thing we're asking, for I'm quite a weight—

he'll really be carrying two people instead of one, and he doesn't look very strong.'

Ezra was amazed, for no one had ever spoken like that before. He twitched his tail and turned his head suspiciously to watch as Mary walked towards him. She walked steadily with her hand out, trusting.

'She's a fool,' Ezra thought. He opened his mouth and bared his teeth ready to snap and then, for some reason, he closed it again. Mary laid a hand on his head. Ezra flinched at the touch, but did not move away.

'Please,' Mary said. 'Would you take us to Bethlehem? I know it's a long way and we'll all get very tired before we get there, but we've got to make the journey. We've no choice. But you have. You must only take us if you want to.'

Ezra shifted slightly.

'Careful, Mary,' Joseph warned.

Gently, she touched one of the donkey's long, grey ears. 'You need only take us if you really want to,' she said again.

Afterwards, Ezra could never explain why it was that he stood quietly and patiently as Joseph lifted Mary on to his back. She leaned forwards and stroked his neck.

'What's his name?' she asked.

'Ezra,' said his master. He shook his head in

amazement. 'Well, I must say I'm dumbfounded. I've never seen him like that before.' He took the money that Joseph offered, and again shook his head. 'I just hope it's not one of his tricks and he doesn't bolt off with the lady on his back. Here,' he said, and gave Joseph his stout stick. 'You give him a clout with that from time to time. It'll remind him who's boss.'

Mary bent down and spoke into Ezra's ear. 'Well Ezra,' she said. 'Shall we go?'

And Ezra lowered his head, walked out of his master's stable and began the long walk to Bethlehem.

They walked until late into the night. They walked until the moon was high and the stars were out. And, as they walked, Mary talked to the donkey. She told him about her life and about an angel who had come to tell her that her baby would be special. Her baby, who would be God's son. Ezra listened and walked carefully along the rough road, picking his way in order that Mary should have a smooth ride.

At last they stopped and Joseph lifted Mary from his back. 'We must eat and sleep. Are you very tired?'

'Not really,' she said. Then she turned and kissed Ezra's nose. 'Thank you.'

They ate their own supper in a hollow near to the road and fed Ezra with oats and carrots. Ezra watched them for a while, then wandered away. He looked around and could see, by the light of the moon, a landscape of bare scrub dotted with large boulders and scrawny trees. He looked back at Mary and Joseph. They had finished eating now and were talking quietly together. Ezra could hear the murmur of their voices, a comforting sound in the empty countryside. Then he heard their laughter and he was suddenly filled with a great sadness. No one, animal or person, had ever laughed with him. He watched as Mary settled herself to sleep and Joseph tucked a blanket around her before lying down himself.

No one, Ezra thought, from the time he had been taken from his mother, had ever said a kind word or

shown him any love. He felt a sudden rush of tears, and shook them away for he was a crusty old donkey who never cried. He moved away and, as he did so, realized that he was neither tethered nor bound. He was free. Free to go and find fields of grass and clover, free to wander, to run, to kick up his heels. He took another step, then turned once more to look at Mary and Joseph, now lying side by side.

'But don't I owe them something?' he found himself thinking. 'She was kind to me, wasn't she, and she talked to me and kissed me and gave me a carrot. What will they do if I leave?'

He shook his head. 'What's a kind voice and a gentle hand and a carrot after all?' he said severely. 'Bribery, that's what. That girl's got you eating out of the palm of her hand. They'll manage if you leave them, they'll be all right. Someone will come along in the morning and give them a lift. They don't need you.' But still he hesitated.

'Just think,' he said to himself. 'Just think, Ezra, what it'll mean if you do stay. We get to Bethlehem, stay a day or two, then make the long journey back to Nazareth. And what lies at the end? What thanks do I get, what reward do I get for staying? Slavery, that's what. Kicks and curses and heavy loads to carry. I'd have lost my one chance of freedom. No. I'd be a fool to stay!'

He gave them one final look. Mary lay in Joseph's arms. They were both asleep and looked innocent and defenceless. For a long while he stood and watched them. Then he sighed and, slowly and heavily, returned to the hollow where they lay. Gently, he nudged Mary's shoulder with his soft nose. She stirred, but did not wake. Ezra sighed again, then stood over them, silently guarding and protecting, all through the long, dark night. He had made his choice.

So Ezra, the worst-tempered donkey in the whole of Israel, plodded, without a grumble or a word of complaint, the long miles to Bethlehem, carrying Mary on his back. And there, in the stable, he had his reward, for he was one of the first to see the miracle of Jesus' birth. And at the sight, the donkey bowed his head and cried with joy.

3
THE BATS FIND A HOME

The trouble started when the family of long-eared bats moved into No. 48.

'This'll be a nice roost for us,' said Mrs Bat, poking about in the loft. 'Very convenient. There'll be plenty of insects in the garden and in those fields beyond.'

Their last home had been in a hollow tree in some woodland, but the trees had been cut down to make way for a road and the bats had been searching for a new home ever since.

'I don't know if this is exactly what we're looking for,' said Mr Bat, doubtfully.

'It's a lot better than some of the places we've seen,' Mrs Bat reminded him. 'Do you remember that semi-detached house a few miles away? The one with the lights in the loft?'

'It would have been much too bright for my eyes,' said Aunt Mabel.

'And what about that house just down the road? The one with the model railway in the attic?'

'We'd have been disturbed all the time, my dear,' said Aunt Mabel. 'Especially when we're trying to have our winter sleep. I *do* like an undisturbed winter sleep.'

Mr Bat, meanwhile, had been flying up and down on a tour of inspection.

'Do you think,' he asked anxiously, 'that we'll be welcome? There are a lot of people who wouldn't like the idea of bats living in their loft.' Mr Bat tended to look on the gloomy side of things.

'Of course they'll like us,' said Mrs Bat, who always looked on the bright side of things. 'We're clean and tidy, and we'll be no trouble. They probably won't even know we're here.'

'We'll be as quiet as mice,' said Uncle Cyril, nodding agreement.

'A *lot* quieter I would hope,' said Mrs Bat sternly. She liked to be accurate. 'You can hear mice coming for miles around—a terrible noise they make.'

'That's only because you've specially good hearing, my dear,' said Aunt Mabel.

'*All* my family have good hearing, I'm pleased to say,' said Mrs Bat.

Great-Uncle Alfred, the head of the family, suddenly spoke. 'I like this loft,' he said. 'I like roosting high up. It's safer than on the ground.'

'Foxes,' said Great-Aunt Hortensia in her high, squeaky voice. Great-Aunt Hortensia was twenty years old (a great age for a bat) and never spoke more than one word at a time.

Everyone nodded solemnly. They all knew about foxes. Two of their family had recently been eaten by foxes when roosting in a hole near the ground.

Mrs Bat flew noiselessly round the loft. 'Yes,' she said at last, 'I like this place too. It'll be a good roost in which to bring up the children.'

And so the entire family—aunts, uncles, great-aunts, great-uncles, cousins, children and all—moved into No. 48.

At first, everything went well. The family who lived in the house were unaware of their new lodgers. The bats flew soundlessly in and out at night through a small hole just under the eaves. There was a good supply of insects from the garden and the fields at the back of the house, the loft was dark and there were plenty of beams from which to hang.

'I'm very happy here,' said Mrs Bat contentedly, while retrieving a baby bat that was wandering too far.

'Pity about the noise,' said Mr Bat sourly, for the son of the owners of No. 48—whose surname was Treacle—wanted to be a pop star and practised loudly every night.

'Well, you can't have everything,' said Mrs Bat, tolerantly.

Spring turned into summer and the loft, which had been comfortably warm, suddenly grew uncomfortably warm. The baby bats felt the heat and began crawling out of the loft in search of cooler places. Unfortunately, one of the coolest places they could find was inside Mr and Mrs Treacle's wardrobe.

One day, Mrs Treacle opened the wardrobe door to discover six baby bats hanging from the coat rail!

It was hard to know who was the more frightened. Mrs Treacle screamed, the baby bats squeaked, and Mrs Bat, hearing the commotion, flew into the bedroom to rescue her children. Fortunately, Mrs Treacle fainted, so the bats were able to retreat to the safety of the loft.

'If I've told you once, I've told you a hundred times: you must not leave this loft!' said Mrs Bat sternly to her children.

'But it's too hot here, mum,' Bertie whined.

'You'll just have to put up with it,' she said. 'Goodness knows the trouble we had to find this place. It's a lot better than some roosts, I can tell you, and the best thing of all is that it's safe—so just remember that, and stay here until you're old enough to fly!'

But the loft was safe no longer. When Mrs Treacle recovered, she telephoned her husband at work and told him of her fright.

'Rats, did you say?' he asked.

'No, not rats—*bats*,' she said. 'In the wardrobe!'

'Whatever were they doing in the wardrobe?' Mr Treacle asked.

'Hanging,' Mrs Treacle said. 'From the rail.'

'Why were they doing that?'

'I didn't stop to ask them,' replied Mrs Treacle, icily. 'But whatever they're doing, they've *got* to be got rid of. I *won't* have bats in the house. Nasty, dirty things, you don't know where they've been. She shuddered. 'Just looking at them makes me go all funny. You'll have to do something about it.'

Mr Treacle sighed. He didn't much like the thought of bats either.

When Mr Treacle arrived home, he climbed into the loft and switched on the light. He looked around, but he could not see anything, for bats can keep very quiet and very still.

'There's nothing there,' he said, climbing down from the loft. 'Perhaps they just happened to get stuck in the wardrobe on their way to somewhere else.'

Mrs Treacle was not so sure, but as she did not want to go into the loft herself, and as there was no trace of bats anywhere else in the house, she had to be content.

Mr and Mrs Bat made quite sure that their children did not stray from the loft until they could fly, and the summer passed quietly.

The weather turned colder, the loft cooled down and, one by one, the bats began their long winter sleep. In December, Mr and Mrs Treacle and their son went away. They left the central heating on and opened the trapdoor to the loft, so that the water tank would not freeze. Then they packed their cases, locked the front door, and flew away for a winter holiday in the sun.

The warmth from the central heating rose into the

loft and one by one the bats began to wake up.

'Is it spring, mum?' asked Bertie.

'I don't know, dear,' said his mother. 'It's certainly warm, but somehow I don't feel as if I've been asleep long enough.'

'Something odd's happening,' said Mr Bat.

'It's all to do with global warming,' said Uncle Cyril briskly. Uncle Cyril prided himself on his general knowledge. 'The earth's warming up.'

'However do you know that?' asked Mrs Bat, admiringly.

'I keep my ears open,' said Uncle Cyril, flapping back his long ears.

'Can we go and explore?' asked the children. 'The trapdoor's open.'

'Well…' said Mrs Bat, doubtfully. 'If you're very, very careful, and come straight back if you hear any noise.'

A stream of small bats flew out of the trapdoor. Unfortunately, they left the loft just as the Treacle family arrived home from their holiday, and they all met in the hall. The family shrieked, the bats squeaked and flew straight back through the trap-door.

'There,' said Mrs Treacle with satisfaction. 'I told you so.' And, for the second time, she fainted.

'Why don't people like us?' asked Bertie, once the

bats were safely back in the loft.

Mrs Bat waved her wings. 'I don't know. Perhaps because we're dark and we fly by night.'

'I can tell you why,' said Uncle Cyril. 'It's because of our distant relatives, the vampire bats—you know, the ones that live in South America and feed on blood. People think all bats are the same.'

'People have never liked us,' said Mr Bat gloomily. 'And now it looks as if we're going to lose our home.'

But Mr Treacle was finding it harder than he supposed to get rid of his unwanted guests.

'Sorry,' said the rodent officer he telephoned. 'Bats are an endangered species and protected by law.'

'What do you mean?' asked Mr Treacle.

'They can't be harmed,' said the rodent officer.

'What do you mean, they can't be harmed? They're harming my wife. She's having hysterics on the sofa.'

'Sorry,' said the rodent officer. 'You'll just have to put up with them.'

'Well I'm sorry too', said Mr Treacle. 'But those bats have GOT TO GO!'

'In that case, you'll need to find a rodent officer who is licensed as an official bat remover. He'll come and move them for you.'

'Why didn't you say so the first time?' asked Mr Treacle.

Up in the loft, meanwhile, the bats were holding a conference.

'They can't get rid of us, I tell you,' said Uncle Cyril. 'We're protected by law.'

'That's as maybe,' said Mr Bat, 'but if they want us out, they'll get us out, protected or not.'

'I don't trust that boy of theirs,' said Aunt Mabel. 'All that terrible music he plays and as for his singing... well!'

'I vote we move now, before it's too late,' said Mr Bat.

'But it took us so long to find this roost,' Mrs Bat said, 'and it's been so comfortable.'

'Oh let's go somewhere else, Mum,' Bertie said, eagerly. 'I'm bored here.'

Great-Uncle Alfred, who had been silent during the discussion, suddenly spoke. 'I think we should leave,' he said. 'You can't be too careful where humans are concerned. They might take it into their heads to get rid of us, protected or not, and then where would we be?'

'Dead,' said Great-Aunt Hortensia, and that settled the argument. The bats would move.

So that night they rose up and, looking like a great cloud of black smoke, streamed out of the loft and into the night.

When the licensed bat remover arrived at No. 48

he found that he had no bats to move.

'Lucky for you they went of their own accord,' he told Mr and Mrs Treacle. 'Sometimes bats get so attached to their roosts that they return time and time again, even though we've moved them miles away.'

For a third time Mrs Treacle fainted.

The bats, meanwhile, were flying round the village, listening and watching for a good place in which to roost. They flew over the new housing estate, circled the pub and crossed the village green. The great, grey-stone building of the church stood before them.

Great-Uncle Alfred paused in flight. 'Listen,' he said.

The bats listened.

'Singing,' said Mrs Bat.

'Best avoid it,' said Mr Bat, nervously.

Uncle Cyril agreed. 'Might be like the last roost,' he said. 'Now I like a good tuneful song, but the noise that Treacle lad made was awful.'

'I rather liked it,' said Bertie.

'You would,' said Uncle Cyril.

But Great-Uncle Alfred was already flying towards the church. 'I think this could be just what we're looking for,' he said happily. 'Follow me.'

The bats entered through a hole just under the roof. The church was full of people and the singing was loud and clear.

'Just look at that tree,' said Bertie, staring down at the brightly lit Christmas tree beneath him.

'Just look at those people,' said Mr Bat nervously. 'Why are they singing?'

Great-Uncle Alfred settled on an oak beam. 'Because they are happy,' he said.

'Why are they happy?' asked Mr Bat suspiciously.

'Because they are celebrating the birthday of Jesus,' said Great-Uncle Alfred. 'Listen.'

And, as the bats listened, they could hear other voices mingling with the singers in church. Pure, high voices which seemed to come from the air itself. The bats, with their sensitive ears, could hear the angels singing with the congregation as they welcomed Christmas Day.

Uncle Cyril nodded his head. 'This'll be a safe roost for us,' he said.

'Safe,' echoed Great-Aunt Hortensia, folding her wings. And that settled the matter.

4

THE LONELY SHEEP

One cold winter's night, three shepherds sat huddled over a fire near the entrance to the sheepfold. They were watching over their sheep. Their flock huddled together in another corner and watched the shepherds.

'All right for them,' said one of the sheep, eyeing the shepherds enviously. 'Nice and cosy round that fire.'

'We could always go a bit nearer,' murmured a second sheep.

'And be shoo-ed away? Not likely.'

A third sheep sighed. 'Who'd be a sheep? I mean, just look at us. Silly tails and small heads.'

'My head's not small,' the second sheep objected. 'And my tail's very nice, I'll have you know.'

'Oh come on,' jeered the third sheep. 'We look ridiculous!'

'Well, I'd rather be a sheep than one of them,' said the first sheep, nodding her head towards the shepherds. Everyone fell silent.

'Do you think,' said the third sheep, 'that it was some kind of joke on God's part?'

'What was?' asked the first sheep.

'Making us. Sheep. So that God could have a good laugh?'

'Maybe,' said the first sheep.

'But surely we were made for a reason?' said a quiet voice. It came from a small sheep standing under a tree a short distance away.

The other sheep looked at her for a moment, then huddled closer together.

'Well, God may have made us sheep as a sort of joke,' said a fourth sheep quietly, 'but I'm very thankful I'm not like *that*...' and she nodded in the direction of the sheep who stood by herself.

'So am I,' agreed the first sheep.

The small sheep looked at the shepherds. It must be nice and warm over there, she thought. But she did not envy the shepherds their fire. They had a hard life out in the fields.

The wind blew and the small sheep shivered. The ground was frozen and there was a sharp nip in the air that spoke of snow to come. It would be warmer huddled close to the other sheep, but she did not try

to join them. If she did, they would either drift away to a different part of the fold or push her off with their hard heads. It was not worth the effort.

From the moment she had been born she had known she was different. None of the other lambs would play with her. 'Go away,' they had said, when she had tried to join in their running and jumping games. 'We don't want you.'

'Why?' she had asked, but no one would tell her.

She had tried asking her mother, but her mother only turned away from her in silence. She had tried asking the other sheep, but they only jeered at her and called her names. She had even tried asking the cows in the next field, but they only lifted their noses disdainfully and would not reply. So she had grown up keeping to a different side of the field. She was small because she ate only the poorer grass. The best grass was eaten by the rest of the flock.

'If only the other sheep would talk to me,' she thought. 'Just once. If only I could huddle close to them and feel part of the flock, instead of always being on my own.'

Time passed and it grew dark. The flock was quiet and still and the shepherds, too, were silent, dozing contentedly beside their fire. A thick white frost covered the field.

Then a voice spoke out of the black night sky, and the field was suddenly bathed in a golden light. The small sheep listened, entranced.

The voice stopped speaking, the light faded, and the small sheep left the shelter of the tree.

'Might as well go and see what all the fuss is about,' she thought. 'No one will miss me.'

She began crossing the field, which looked white and mysterious under its coating of frost.

'Who knows,' she thought as she nimbly jumped through a gap in the stone wall, 'there might even be a place for me in the stable the voice talked about. Perhaps, if I can find it, I won't be lonely any more.'

Reuben, the youngest of the shepherds, had also seen the light and heard the angel's voice. He turned to his companions.

'Elias! Joshua! Did you see that?'

The shepherds stirred.

'What…? What's happening?' asked Joshua.

'Someone been after the sheep?' asked Elias.

'I don't know,' said Reuben. 'I heard a voice… and saw a light…'

Joshua looked round. 'There's no light here. It's pitch dark. I reckon you been dreamin'.'

Reuben shook his head. 'I wasn't. I heard a voice. It talked about a baby… a newborn baby…'

'Well, I heard somethin' too,' said Elias, 'but I reckoned I been dreamin'. After all, what would someone be doing in the middle of a field, in the middle of the night, in the middle of winter, talkin' about a newborn baby?' he went on, scornfully. 'Don't make sense!'

'Anyway, babies is nothin' new,' said Joshua. 'There's babies bein' born every minute.'

'But this is a wonderful baby,' Reuben insisted. 'The Saviour of the world… that's what the voice said. It's a miracle!'

'Well, I don't want to see no miracles,' said Joshua firmly. 'I don't believe in them. You've been asleep an' havin' a bad dream.' With that he lay down and closed his eyes.

'Perhaps I have,' said Reuben doubtfully. 'The

voice said something about going to Bethlehem...' he looked across the field, and that was when he discovered the missing sheep.

By now, the small sheep was far away. She had trudged across field after field. The going had been hard and the sheep was tired and thirsty. She stopped and looked around. Below her lay a pool of still, clear water. Above her, the sky was black, with a mass of white stars. Everywhere was very quiet, and very still.

'I'll just have a drink at that pool,' she thought, 'and then I'll go on'.

She clambered down the bank and bent her head to drink. She could see stars reflected in the still water. She could see white, frost-covered hills. She could see her eyes, glowing. But she could not see her face. Where there should have been a reflection of her face mirrored in the dark waters of the pool, she could see—nothing. For a long moment she stared, then she lifted her head.

'So that's why I'm different,' she thought. 'Now I know.'

The small sheep took another step... and slipped down the bank and into the pool. A moment later she was floundering in the water, her legs tangled in thick weeds.

'Help!' she called in fright. 'Ba-aa! Ba-aa! Help!!'

The sheep were grumbling as the shepherds drove them through the gap in the stone wall.

'It's a bit much taking us on a route march at this time of the night,' said the first sheep.

'Especially after *that* sheep,' said the second. 'Who cares if she's gone missing?'

'She might have been stolen,' said the third sheep.

'Who'd want to steal her?' asked the first sheep, sourly.

'Perhaps,' said the fourth sheep, who had been rather quiet and thoughtful since they had heard the news, 'perhaps she just went off because we've not been very kind to her.'

The rest of the flock looked at one another uncomfortably and fell silent.

As the shepherds drove their flock across the fields in search of the lost sheep, the small, lonely sheep, who had crossed the fields in search of someone who would want her, stopped struggling. She was cold right through and just wanted to sleep.

For one last time she cried out, 'Baa-aa... Baa-aa... Help me...!'

And it was that cry that brought the shepherds and their flock running to the pool.

'She needs warmth,' said Reuben, wrapping the small sheep in his cloak.

'There's a stable over there,' said Elias.

So Reuben carried the small sheep to the stable. The door was open and light and warmth streamed out. As Reuben entered, the small sheep stirred in his arms and opened her eyes. She saw the shepherds and the sheep staring at her, worried and concerned.

'Perhaps,' she thought, 'they do want me, after all,' and a great warmth began to spread through her.

Then she saw the baby, lying in the straw-filled crib. She jumped out of Reuben's arms and ran across the floor to where the baby held out his arms to welcome her—the small black sheep, lonely no longer.

5

THE CHRISTMAS TREE

Deep in the forest, two birds were building a nest in the branches of a thick fir-tree.

'This will be a nice safe home to bring up the chicks,' Mrs Bird said approvingly as she patted the twigs into place.

'That's true,' Mr Bird agreed. 'No one will trouble us here.'

They finished building their nest, lining it with feathers and soft, mossy grass for comfort and warmth and, in due time, Mrs Bird laid three eggs. She sat keeping them warm while her husband flew backwards and forwards bringing her juicy worms to eat. Two of the eggs soon hatched and Mr Bird was kept even busier finding food for the chicks and their mother. But the third egg did not hatch, despite all Mrs Bird's attempts to keep it warm.

The baby chicks grew up and took their first wobbly

flights to the safety of a nearby branch. As they grew stronger they began searching for food for themselves, flying further each day until at last they flew from the nest altogether, leaving Mr and Mrs Bird alone, apart from the third egg, which still had not hatched.

It started to rain and the wind turned cold.

'Perhaps we should move somewhere warmer,' Mr Bird suggested, as he watched the rain spatter ceaselessly down through the trees in the forest.

Mrs Bird shook her head. 'I'm not moving until my third egg has hatched,' she said firmly.

'But my dear wife,' said Mr Bird gently, 'my very dearest wife, I'm very much afraid that our third egg is not going to hatch at all.'

'Nonsense,' said Mrs Bird. However, she could not help thinking that her husband was right as the days grew darker and the first snows of winter began to fall—and still the third egg did not hatch. So one day she rose sadly from the egg and, after giving it a little farewell peck with her beak, she and her husband flew away.

They were only just in time, for the forest was suddenly filled with noise. There were sounds of large motor vehicles, crashing feet, shouting people, while over it all rose the whine and shriek of a chainsaw. The two birds trembled as they hovered high above their old nest.

'Whatever's happening?' they asked, as they looked down at the forest. With a terrible sound the fir-tree crashed to the ground and the whole forest shook.

'Come away, come away!' shouted Mr Bird, but Mrs Bird swooped down and circled the tree crying, 'My egg, oh my egg! I shouldn't have left you!'

It was almost dark by the time the men had finished cutting down the trees. They loaded them on to lorries and drove away, and no one noticed the two small birds who flew behind.

'Where are we going?' asked Mr Bird, trying to keep up with his wife.

'To find my egg,' his wife said, determinedly.

The trees were taken to a town and left in the market square, and Mr and Mrs Bird spent the night flying in and out of the dark branches of their old home, trying vainly to find their nest.

'My poor egg will be so frightened,' said Mrs Bird as the first streaks of dawn appeared. Her husband sighed and said nothing.

People came early in the morning to buy the Christmas trees and Mr and Mrs Bird saw their fir-tree tied to the roof of a car and driven away.

'Come on,' said Mrs Bird briskly.

'Must we?' asked Mr Bird wearily, but he followed his wife, and his wife followed the car. At last it stopped outside a house, and the birds watched as the fir-tree was carried indoors.

'Well, that's that,' said Mr Bird. 'We've done all we can. We might as well fly south now.'

His wife shook her head. 'My egg might need me,' she said simply.

'Of course it won't,' Mr Bird said, somewhat irritably. 'Dearest wife, how many times do I have to tell you? The egg never hatched. There *is* no chick. *Please* let us fly south.' But Mrs Bird refused to go. She flew to the window of the house and peered inside. Then she gasped.

'Just look,' she said. 'Look what they've done to our tree!'

Mr Bird looked, and he too gasped in amazement.

For the tree which had been their home for so many months was transformed, decked out in a blaze of tiny lights which winked and twinkled, shining like brilliant stars among the dark green pine needles. Silver and gold balls danced from the tips of the branches, and the entire tree was clothed in thin silver threads which sparkled and shimmered.

'It's magic!' breathed Mr Bird.

Mrs Bird, for once, was speechless. She stared and stared at the tree, and at last she said, 'They've decorated it because of my egg. Something wonderful is going to happen. A miracle. Just you wait and see.'

'No such thing as miracles,' said Mr Bird, but he said it quietly.

So the two birds stayed in the garden, watching and waiting. Each night they slept in the bare branches of an apple tree, huddled close together for warmth, and each day they peered through the window, staring in wonder at the fir-tree, which continued to shine gloriously. Presents were piled beneath it and every evening the family sat round, their faces glowing in the fire-light, while the tree also seemed to glow, lit by the fires reflected in the gold and silver balls. Then the presents were opened and the tree stood amid a discarded mound of paper wrapping, still proudly shining. And the birds continued to watch and wait.

'Perhaps now something wonderful will happen,' said Mrs Bird hopefully. 'Perhaps now my egg will hatch.'

But then came the day when the birds saw the tree stripped of its finery. The silver threads, the gold and silver balls, the bright lights were all carefully taken down and packed into boxes.

'Whatever are they doing?' asked Mrs Bird. Mr Bird shook his head.

The back door opened and the tree was carried out and dumped beside the fence.

'Why have they thrown it away?' asked Mrs Bird, staring at it in dismay.

'Perhaps they've no further use for it,' said Mr Bird.

'Well, I call that downright wasteful,' said Mrs Bird.

'Oh I don't know,' said Mr Bird. 'It gave the people in the house pleasure for a time, just as it gave us shelter and a home for a time. That's not a waste.' He was silent for a while, then he sighed. 'I'm afraid, my dear, that nothing very wonderful is going to happen now.'

Mrs Bird flew to the fence and looked down at the tree. 'No,' she said at last. 'Nothing wonderful *is* going to happen. You were right, of course, and I was just being silly. Let's fly away south.'

But as soon as she had finished speaking there came a sudden, sharp cracking sound. Mrs Bird

swooped down from the fence and Mr Bird swooped after her. And there, deep inside the tree, warmed by the many tiny lights which had surrounded it, the third egg finally hatched and a hungry chick called loudly for food.

'Who said miracles don't happen?' said Mrs Bird, happily settling herself beside her chick. 'Now go and find some food.'

6

THE ANIMALS' CHRISTMAS

There was a terrible traffic jam at the crossroads in the town of Bethlehem and the ox, tired after his hard day's work in the fields, snorted and stamped his feet irritably as he waited to return to his stable. When he finally arrived he was not in a good mood.

'I don't know what's happening, I really don't,' he grumbled, as he entered the door. 'The town's gone mad—people, animals, I never saw the like! Do you know, it took me all of half an hour to get here from the field? Half an hour! And the noise! Dreadful...' the ox stopped abruptly as he stared round the stable. 'Here—what's going on?'

A donkey and two cows were staring back at him from inside the stable.

'What are you doing here?' the ox demanded. 'This is *my* stable, I'll have you know. Mine and my friend's!' He lowered his head angrily. 'So whatever you're doing, I want you out—sharpish!'

'Sorry,' said one of the cows. 'There's nowhere else for us to go.'

'What do you mean, nowhere for you to go?' repeated the ox. 'Of *course* there's places for you to go. There's stables, the whole town's full of stables, half empty most of them! You can't have tried!'

'We have. My master's been round everywhere. Quite walked us off our feet, but this is the last stable with any room to spare.'

'What's wrong with the fields then?' said the ox, stubbornly. 'You cows are used to being out in the fields. Why don't you spend the night in the fields?'

'It's too cold out there.'

'Cold? Huh! Toughen you up,' said the ox.

The ox's companion pushed his nose over the edge of his partition.

'What's going on in the town?' he asked mildly.

'Yes,' asked one of the cows. 'What *is* going on? Why's Bethlehem so popular all of a sudden? It's not as if it's a holiday resort or a city like Jerusalem.'

'I think it's on account of the census,' said the donkey.

'What's that?'

'The Romans want to count all the people, so they told them to go back to where they were born…'

'Bit of a stupid idea, if you ask me,' said the owl

from her perch high up in the rafters.

'Well, yes,' agreed the donkey, nodding his head, 'but that's Romans for you.'

'It still doesn't explain what you're all doing in my stable,' said the first ox, stubbornly.

'Yes it does,' said the donkey. 'The town's full, so we've been asked to share.'

'Nobody asked me,' said the ox crossly.

Just then the stable door burst open.

'Oh close that door, for goodness' sake,' the owl called down. 'There's a terrible draught!'

A goat stood just inside the door, looked round and blinked. 'Sorry,' she bleated.

'I suppose you're another one,' said the ox.

'Another what?' asked the goat.

'Another one who thinks they can share my stable tonight.'

'Well, yes,' said the goat.

'Then you've got another think coming,' said the ox, lowering his head dangerously.

'Oh don't be so silly,' said the goat. 'This is the only place with a bit of warmth. My beard's frozen stiff!'

'You'll have more than a frozen beard if you don't clear out,' threatened the ox. 'There's no room.'

'There's plenty of room,' said the goat.

'I don't care if there's all the room in the world!' shouted the ox. 'This is *my* stable!'

'It's not your stable,' said a mouse, running across the floor. 'I live here as well.'

'So do I,' hooted the owl. 'Only I don't make a fuss about it.'

'It's my home too,' said a rat quietly, slinking through the straw.

'And mine,' whispered a spider from the middle of her web.

'Mine too,' said a flea, jumping on the ox's back.

'Oh get off!' said the ox, crossly. 'What I mean is, I won't have strangers coming in!'

'Just as well I'm not a stranger then,' said the innkeeper's cat, jumping in through the window. The mouse shrieked and ran for cover as the door opened once more, this time admitting a horse.

'Shut that door!' commanded the owl.

The horse looked round the stable, his long nose quivering. 'Well really,' he said in a complaining voice. 'This is not the kind of accommodation I'm used to'.

'In that case, why don't you shove off?' said the ox rudely.

'And close the door behind you,' added the owl.

'I'm used to a stall to myself,' said the horse, 'with good fresh hay and a warm blanket to keep out the cold. And where's my bran feed?'

'We're all stuck here for the night,' said the goat, 'so we'd better make the best of it.'

'Well *I'm* not prepared to make the best of it,' said the ox firmly. 'You seem to forget it's *my* stable you're in!'

'And mine,' said the quiet ox. 'But I'm not complaining. After all, it's nice to talk to other animals. It gets a bit boring talking to you all the time.'

'Me?' gasped the first ox. 'Boring? Why you... you...' He lowered his head to charge.

'Now stop that!' said one of the cows. 'I can't take violence. It upsets me and as I'm expecting a baby...'

'That'll make it even more crowded,' giggled the goat.

The cat chuckled. 'If you think this is crowded, you should see the inn! At least two to a bed, and they're beginning to sleep in the corridors. And the noise! You wouldn't believe the noise that people can make. That's why I've come here—for a bit of peace and quiet.'

'It doesn't seem like there's going to be much peace in here tonight,' said the donkey dryly, 'and as for quiet...'

'FOR THE LAST TIME, WILL YOU ALL GET OUT!' shouted the ox.

'NO!' the other animals roared back. The cows mooed, the donkey brayed, the goat bleated, the owl hooted, and the mouse brought his excited family in to watch the fun,

'Good as a circus it is, but mind, we must make a quick exit if a fight begins,' the mouse told his family. 'And watch out for that cat!'

'I say!' said the horse. 'I say, this just isn't fair!'

'I wish you wouldn't always get so angry,' the quiet ox said to his friend. 'It doesn't make for a peaceful life.'

But the first ox was not listening. Head down, hooves pawing the earth, he charged. Everyone stepped out of the way and the ox would have hit his head hard against the stable door if it had not suddenly opened. Unable to stop himself, he rushed straight out of the stable, across the courtyard and landed head first in a large pile of hay.

The animals cheered.

A shabby-looking donkey, patiently waiting to come inside, looked round. 'What was that?' he asked.

'Just my friend,' said the quiet ox. 'He tends to get a bit over-excited at times. Take no notice.' He drew himself up to his full height. 'Allow me to welcome you to our stable. I expect you want shelter for the night.'

'Yes,' said the donkey. 'I do. And so do my master and mistress. We've travelled a long way and we're all very tired.'

The donkey entered the stable. On his back was a young girl, who was swaying wearily. An older man followed on foot.

The animals looked at the newcomers.

'Have you come far?' asked the cow.

'From Nazareth.'

'Is that a long way?' demanded the goat.

'Far enough.'

The man helped the girl from the donkey's back.

'Oh look,' said the cow, pleased. 'She's expecting a baby, just like me!'

'Ahh,' said the owl. 'I do like babies. I've been quite lonely since mine have all grown up and flown the nest.'

The man gathered together some straw for a bed

and gently helped the girl lie down. She smiled up at him, then closed her eyes.

'I say,' said the horse, 'those humans can't stay here!'

'Oh don't you start!,' said the quiet ox. 'There's plenty of room.'

'I didn't mean that,' said the horse. 'I mean, it's not right. Not right at all! Stables are for animals. Humans live in houses.'

There was a furious pounding on the door.

'That'll be the ox,' sighed the goat. 'I wouldn't let him in if I were you.'

'But it's his stable as well as mine,' said the quiet ox, mildly.

The ox burst in, then stopped in astonishment. 'What on earth's going on now?'

'I think,' said the owl, who had flown down from the rafters. 'That the girl is having a baby. *Do* close the door, and *try* not to be more of a nuisance than you are already.'

'Humans?' spluttered the ox. 'Staying in *my* stable?' He shook his head. 'Well, I'm speechless!'

'Thank goodness for that,' said the goat.

It was peaceful in the stable as the baby was born. The only sounds to be heard were the breathing of the animals, the odd rustle of the straw, and the flutter of wings as the owl flew back and forth.

At last, the baby gave a cry and the animals drew near the rough crib in which he lay. Then, as the baby opened his eyes, the animals sank to their knees.

'This,' said the cow, 'is no ordinary baby.'

Everyone was silent, even the ox. But after a while, the peace was broken by a loud banging. The door burst open and in walked three shepherds, followed by their sheep.

'Well really!' exclaimed the ox. 'Without a "by your leave" or a "would you mind?" Some people have no manners!'

But he no longer sounded cross. Neither did the owl, who ruffled her feathers as she said, 'Close that door, we don't want the baby to catch cold!'

7

THE KOALA'S SPECIAL DAY

The koala bear opened first one eye, then the other. He yawned, stretched and sat up so quickly that he fell off the branch of the eucalyptus tree where he had been sleeping. Rubbing his bruised behind, he wondered what had woken him up. He usually slept for most of the day, unless he was hungry.

Why *had* he woken up? He sniffed the air. The forest did not *smell* any different. He looked around. It did not *look* any different either. Then he felt it. From the tips of his large furry ears to the bottom of his big feet, the koala sensed that today was going to be a good day. Today something wonderful was going to happen.

'Today is a… is a… a *special* day!' he said out loud to the waking forest.

There was a raucous laugh behind him.

'Every day's a special day,' laughed the kookaburra. 'Only you koalas are usually too fast asleep to notice.'

'I'm not sleepy today,' said the koala. 'I'm wide...
wide...' he yawned loudly, suddenly tired, and
conscious of his bruises. He had fallen a long way.

'Wake up, lazybones!' shouted the kookaburra in
his ear.

'I'm not lazy, I'm just sleepy...' the koala yawned
again, 'and I fell out of the tree. That's a tiring thing
to happen to anyone.'

'Well I can't stay here nattering,' said the kookaburra. 'Some of us have work to do.' She flapped her
wings, ready to fly off.

'Wait a minute,' the koala called. 'Don't go just yet.
There's something I want to ask you.'

The kookaburra stood poised for flight. 'Well?'

The koala took a deep breath. 'It's this feeling I've
got. I'm sure something exciting's going to happen.
Do you feel it too?'

'Me?' The kookaburra flapped her wings again
and laughed. 'Naw.' And she flew away. The koala
screwed his eyes against the bright morning light and
watched her go.

'Oh well.' He looked up at the eucalyptus tree and
thought he would like to eat a tasty leaf or two before
curling up once more on one of the branches and
going back to sleep. The excited feeling was still there,
but it was so hot and sticky in the forest and thinking
took so much effort...

A shower of earth spattered over him. Then another. There was a snuffling sound and the koala saw a short, stubby tail emerging from a hole. The rest of the animal followed. It was a hairy-nosed wombat who, having climbed out, reached down and helped his wife and two baby wombats to the surface. He looked around and sniffed the air.

'Where am I?'

'In the forest,' said the koala.

The wombat tut-tutted. 'I know *that*, but *where* in the forest?'

'Well...' the koala stopped. 'I don't know *where*. The forest is the forest.'

The wombat frowned. 'I received the invitation and began burrowing at once, but I'm not sure I'm in the right place. Is this the right place?'

'It all depends on where you want to be,' replied the koala.

'Oh. The instructions *seemed* clear enough...' the wombat began, looking worried.

'Yes, but you're very bad at following directions, dear,' said his wife. 'Especially underground.'

'Hmm. Well, I'm very sorry to have bothered you.' He turned to his wife and children. 'Come along. Back into the hole.'

'Wait a minute!' It was the kookaburra. She flew down and perched on a pile of earth.

'Yes?'

'I wouldn't go *too* far, if you get my meaning.'

The wombat looked puzzled for a moment, then his face cleared. 'Oh! Oh, I *see*! Right. Well, thank you. Thank you!' And he and his family disappeared inside the hole.

'What was that about?' asked the koala, puzzled.

The kookaburra laughed. 'Oh nothing. Just wombats. You know what *they're* like. Bury their heads so far in the earth that they can't see what's in front of their noses!' She screeched with laughter. 'Get it? Heads in the earth... oh never mind. Perhaps it wasn't funny after all.'

The koala's face cleared. 'I've got it!' he said suddenly.

'Oh really?' The kookaburra looked quite pleased. 'I didn't think it was a bad joke myself.'

'I know what the excited feeling's about. It's my *birthday*!'

The kookaburra began preening her feathers. 'Is that all?'

'It's the day I was born!'

'Birthdays usually are.'

'But it's special!'

The wombat popped his head out of the hole. 'Don't see what's so special about that,' he said. 'We all have birthdays. Every year. Mine comes round regular as clockwork. Depressing when you're as old as I am.'

'Yes, but...' the koala began. 'But...' He yawned again. He wanted to explain that when you're only one year old, and you've spent half of that year living inside your mother's pouch, having a birthday was something special. Something to be celebrated. But it all seemed so complicated and much too much effort, and it was so hot, and he was so tired. The excited feeling seemed to be draining away... Then he saw his mother sitting high up in a tree, eating a breakfast of eucalyptus.

'Mother,' he called. 'Mother!'

'Yes, dear?' she said, in between mouthfuls.

'It's my birthday today,' he said, climbing up to join her.

'I know that,' she said placidly, continuing to eat.

'Well, isn't it exciting?'

'I don't know that it's anything to get worked up about,' she said.

'Oh.' The koala sighed. The excited feeling inside him had nearly all gone.

There was a thud, thudding in the undergrowth and two red kangaroos came crashing through the trees.

'Hey, we heard there was a party, do you know where it is?'

'A party?' asked the koala.

'Sure. A birthday party,' the second one explained. 'Owwh! What did you do that for?' he asked, for the first kangaroo had stamped heavily on his foot.

The excited feeling rushed over the koala bear. 'Well, actually it's, it's *my* birthday today,' he began. 'But I don't know about any parties...' his voice trailed off, for the first kangaroo was shaking his head.

'No. Can't be yours. This is a Christmas party. Sorry about the mistake. Be seein' you.'

Sadly, the koala watched them bound away.

Everyone seemed to be invited to something except him. Perhaps he was still too young to go to parties, even though he was now one year old. He knew all about Christmas, although why it involved a party he couldn't imagine. His mother had told him about the baby Jesus who had been born at Christmas time, but it had happened a long time ago and in a far-off country, so the koala had not been very interested. Christmas seemed to have nothing to do with his life here in the forest.

The air grew hot and still. The wombat burrowed back into his hole, muttering to himself. The kooka-burra flew off. Insects buzzed lazily around the koala's head. His mother disappeared to another eucalyptus tree, and he could see his father swinging lazily from tree to tree. The sun poured down, in and out of the branches, dazzling his eyes, speckling the green leaves with shifting, glinting gold. Everything lay heavy in the heat. The koala could feel the sun speckle his fur with warmth, and his eyes began to close.

So what if it *was* his birthday. No one, apart from himself, seemed to think it special. But it was a shame, though; the excited feeling had been so nice. It had made him feel warm inside, rather like his fur felt in the warmth of the sun. The koala slept...

He woke with a start to find that it was dark. He

stirred and pricked up his ears. There was singing. He moved silently along the branch of the tree. The singing stopped and a voice said:

'Now then, that's not very good. Once more everyone. And put a bit of *feeling* into it.'

He heard the sounds of throats being cleared and then came a chorus of squeaks, grunts and hisses. The koala swung himself down to a lower branch and peered through the tangle of leaves. He could see one of the kangaroos beating time with a stick. What was going on?

'No, no, NO!' The kangaroo threw down his stick angrily. 'Dear, oh dear. Why can't you all sing in key?'

'Us birds can,' said the kookaburra, with a nervous laugh.

'All right,' said the kangaroo wearily 'One more time.'

The koala could remain silent no longer. The excited feeling had returned and it was very strong. He felt wide awake. He swung himself over... and, for the second time that day, fell with a thud to the ground.

'Ouch!' he said, and rubbed the sore place. He looked around. 'What's happening?' he demanded.

Everyone was there. The wombat and his family, his mother and father, his brothers and sisters. The two red kangaroos he had seen earlier in the day were there as well as the kookaburra. And stretching back deep into the forest were all his friends and relations. For a second there was silence. Then his mother spoke: 'It was meant to be a surprise. A surprise party.'

'A *birthday* party,' the wombat added.

'But you said birthdays weren't important,' the koala said.

The wombat scratched his nose. 'Not exactly... I just said they came round regular as clockwork. Anyway, I couldn't say anything else could I? Your ma and pa told me to keep it a secret.'

'And *you* nearly let it out,' said the kangaroo, rounding on his mate. 'You great woolly-footed fool!'

'Sorry,' said the second kangaroo.

'And this is a double birthday party,' said his mother. 'For you were born on Christmas day, the same day as Jesus.'

'Was I?' asked the koala, surprised. Somehow it made the story of Christmas seem much closer.

'Yes,' said his mother, smiling at him. 'You were my special baby, but Jesus was a special baby for the whole world.'

'So let's get on with it then,' said the kookaburra impatiently. 'Let's have a *good* party, because to my mind *all* birthdays are special.'

8
THE CAMELS WHO WENT ROUND IN CIRCLES

The wind was blowing hard across the desert, whipping up the sand and whirling it into the faces of the three camels and their riders. They had travelled a long way and were very tired. They went in single file, the largest camel leading, the smallest at the back. The riders made sure that the precious gifts they were carrying remained well secured, then wrapped their cloaks around their heads to protect them from the sandstorm.

'As if they didn't trust us to carry them and their precious gifts safely,' sniffed the camel in the middle, whose rider was a wise man called Caspar.

The leading camel, who was being ridden by another wise man called Melchior, looked disdainful. 'If *you* were carrying the riches *I* am carrying, you would be glad to know that they were secure. I, after all, am carrying gold to the newborn king. You are carrying only frankincense. A very inferior substance.'

The smallest camel, who was being ridden by the third wise man, Balthazar, said nothing at all. He was carrying myrrh, the least precious of the gifts.

Caspar's camel sneezed suddenly. 'It's all this sand,' he complained. 'Gets right up my nostrils.'

'What do you expect in the desert?' asked Melchior's camel, disagreeably.

The camels and their riders plodded on. The sun set quickly, as it does in the desert, and soon it was quite dark. Melchior's camel stopped suddenly and Caspar's camel bumped into him.

'Whatever do you think you're doing, stopping like that?' he hissed angrily.

'Quiet!' said Melchior's camel. 'I'm thinking.'

'Thinking! Huh! I'm beginning to think it wasn't such a good idea to set off on this wild goose-chase in the first place. And I'm also beginning to wonder whether we'll ever see this king—if there *is* a king; we don't even know that for certain!'

'Nonsense,' said Melchior's camel. 'A wise camel should never have doubts. My master is searching for the baby who is a king in order to give him presents— wonderful and highly expensive presents might I say—and I, being the oldest and wisest of the camels, shall take him there.'

'Well, I think you've got us lost,' said Caspar's camel bluntly.

'I'm following the new star,' Melchior's camel said, loftily. 'That's what my master told me to do.'

'Where is this star then?'

All three camels craned their necks towards the sky. Nothing could be seen for the swirling of dust and sand.

'I vote we stop here for the night—or at least until the storm stops,' said Caspar's camel, stubbornly.

'There's no question of a vote.' Melchior's camel was disdainful. '*I'm* in charge of this expedition, and what I say goes.'

Caspar's camel looked round at the smallest camel.

'What do you say?' he asked.

'Me?' the smallest camel was startled. No one ever asked his opinion. 'Oh, I think we should do what our masters want.'

'Do you hear that?' Caspar's camel chortled. 'Do what our masters want! He's got a lot to learn, hasn't he?'

'In the desert,' said Melchior's camel, grandly, 'we, the camels, are in charge. It is our terrain. We know every hillock and hump. After a pause, he added, 'Our masters only *think* they are in charge.'

With that, he turned and began to walk away into

the night. Grumbling and complaining, Caspar's camel followed. The smallest camel silently brought up the rear.

At last the storm blew itself out. The clouds parted and a starry sky was seen. The leading camel stopped once more.

'I suppose you're thinking again,' said Caspar's camel, sourly.

'That's right.'

All three camels looked up and the smallest camel gasped.

'I've never seen so many stars before.'

'That's just because you've not been around for very long,' said Melchior's camel, in a kind but superior voice. 'When you've seen as many starlit skies as I have you soon learn what's what. You learn to travel by the stars. To understand them. To use them as a guide. Why, I can read the night sky like a chart.'

'If it's all so easy, why don't you stop talking and get on with it, seeing that you don't want us to have a rest,' complained Caspar's camel. 'As far as I'm concerned, I'll be glad to find this king and get home to my oasis. A bit of shade under a palm tree and a nice water-hole would do me very well. Very well indeed.'

The smallest camel said nothing at all, but thought longingly of water, shade and a long, long rest. This was his first journey into the desert.

Despite his talk, Melchior's camel was confused by the sight of so many stars. Some were bright and some were dim, some were large and some were small, but no single star seemed bigger and brighter than the others. However, he was not going to admit it, so they set off again, and for the next day and night they plodded on and on. On the third day Melchior's camel began to go slower and slower.

'What's up?' asked Caspar's camel, suspiciously.

'It's... um... nothing,' said Melchior's camel.

Caspar's camel looked around. 'You know what? I think we've been here before.'

'Nonsense,' said Melchior's camel.

'You're always saying things are nonsense,' said Caspar's camel. 'But it's not nonsense. I recognize that hill over there.'

'Everything shifts and changes in the desert. It's a well-known fact that you can think you're going round in circles whereas in reality...'

'You *are* going round in circles,' Caspar's camel said, accusingly. He stopped and so did the smallest camel. Melchior's camel went on alone for a while, then turned and rejoined the others.

'All right,' he admitted unhappily. 'You're right. We *are* going round in circles.'

Caspar's camel was furious. 'You stupid great animal! Why ever didn't you say so days ago?'

'I'm sorry,' Melchior's camel said, hanging his head.

'Sorry! I should think so. Fine kind of leader you've turned out to be! Get out of the way—I'm in charge now!'

With that, he pushed Melchior's camel to one side. 'Now we'll see a bit of action!' he said, as he turned and headed straight back from where they had just come. With a sigh Melchior's camel fell into second place and the smallest camel, the camel ridden by Balthazar, the youngest and poorest of the wise men, again followed in the rear.

That night the sky was clear and inky black, and studded with thousands upon thousands of stars.

'See,' said Caspar's camel. 'I was right. There's your star. We'll soon find this baby king. I'll be glad to get the weight of the frankincense off my back!'

'What do you think I feel like, weighed down by pure gold?' said Melchior's camel. 'That's far heavier than your incense. And my master, Melchior the Wise, is a good deal fatter than your master, Caspar. A weedy stick of a man your master is, if I might say so. But I don't complain. That's the trouble with you younger camels. Always complaining. You don't catch me complaining.'

The smallest camel said nothing and they all walked on. But as he walked, the smallest camel could not help thinking that the brightest star was not the one they were heading towards, but one that was behind them.

After another day and a night, the three camels and their riders came to a small town.

'I'm sure this is the place,' said Caspar's camel. 'See how well I've led you.'

Thankfully, the three wise men climbed off their camels and went in search of food, rest, and the baby king. They took the precious gifts with them.

'Told you they didn't trust us,' said Caspar's camel.

The three camels also rested and drank greedily from the water-hole. There were other camels there and they began to talk. But as they talked, Caspar's camel's face lengthened. For the other camels were saying that this was not the town that had been spoken of, the one where the baby king was to be found. That lay on the other side of the desert.

'But I've been following the new star so it *must* be the town!' Caspar's camel insisted.

'Sorry, you must have been following an old one,' said the other camels and they lifted up their heads and laughed, for camels like it when others are proved wrong.

The three wise men came back to their camels, tied up the precious gifts and climbed on. Caspar's camel looked at Melchior's.

'Your turn to lead again, I suppose,' he said, 'as I was following the wrong star.'

'But I led you in circles,' said Melchior's camel. 'And I still don't know the way.'

Both camels looked at the smallest camel.

'It's up to you,' they said.

'Me?' said the smallest camel. 'But I'm not old or wise or well-travelled like you.'

'That doesn't seem to count for anything,' said Melchior's camel bitterly.

'Not in the desert,' added Caspar's camel.

So they set off, this time with the smallest camel in the lead. Night fell and the smallest camel looked up at the velvety black sky with its mass of silver stars and marvelled at the bigness of creation.

As he looked, the stars twinkled and gleamed at him. Some of them were large and some were small, but none of them was brighter than the others.

'Oh dear,' said the smallest camel to himself. 'I don't know which is the right star, but I do want to find the baby who's been born a king. My master's gift isn't precious, like gold or frankincense, because he's not a very wealthy man. Myrrh isn't as expensive as the other gifts, but he paid all he could for it and

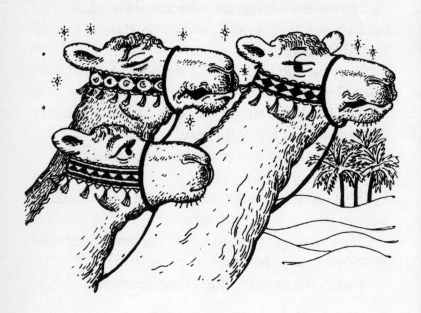

he's come a long way to give it to the baby.'

As he was thinking these thoughts, one star, low on the horizon, began to glow, and as the smallest camel watched, it seemed that it glowed brighter and bigger than all the rest.

The smallest camel began to walk straight towards this star, and the other two camels followed silently. On and on they trudged, right across the desert, Melchior on his camel, Caspar on his, with Balthazar's small camel surely and confidently leading the way.

At last the star came to rest above a stable in a small town and the camels and their riders rode in through the town gates. They entered the stable carrying their precious gifts, the gold, the frankincense and the myrrh, and laid them before the baby. And, as the smallest camel knelt in the straw, he could have sworn that the baby looked at him and smiled.

9

THE CONSTANT GOOSE

The eldest gander stood beside the lake and sniffed the air. It felt sharp and fresh and a keen wind was blowing. He could smell the first snow of winter. Soon the lakes would freeze and the grasslands would disappear under a thick coating of snow. There would be no food and no water. If the geese did not travel soon, it would be too late. He turned to his wife.

'It's time, don't you think?'

The goose nodded sadly. The wide open spaces of the Arctic tundra stretched before her, with its lush green pastures, marshes, ponds, lakes, and thick grass. She would be sorry to leave, but it was indeed time.

The eldest gander called the flock together.

'In three days we travel south,' he announced. 'Eat as much as you can, for the journey is a long and tiring one.'

'Where are we going?' asked the youngest goose, who had been born on the tundra.

'Yes,' echoed the other young geese anxiously, 'where are we going?'

Their father stretched to his full height and opened his wings wide. 'We're flying towards the sun,' he said.

The younger geese looked anxiously at one another.

'There's nothing to be afraid of,' their mother said, comfortingly.

'How do we get there?' the young geese asked.

'Your father knows the way,' said the goose. 'He's made the journey many times.'

The next two days were spent preparing for the flight. The geese made practice runs across the lake.

'We fly in the shape of a "V", so that no one gets lost,' the eldest gander explained. 'It's also less tiring for the younger ones. Everyone has a place. The older ones lead the way, and you youngsters follow. But mind you keep in line, and concentrate on what you're doing, otherwise you'll fall into the ocean and drown.'

On the third day, the flock assembled on the great lake. The eldest gander looked around him. The previous night it had snowed and the tundra was coated with a dusting of white, which sparkled in the

wintry sun. It was indeed time to go.

With a loud cry, he stretched out his neck, spread his wings and rose into the air, and then the quiet of the tundra was filled with the rustle of wings and the cries of the geese as they all rose into the air behind him, formed a perfect 'V', and began the long flight south.

The goose looked down. Below her lay the vast, open plains of her home. She blinked back a tear.

'I'll miss it,' she sighed.

'So will I,' said her husband. 'But we'll be back in the spring.'

Two days later, a weary flock of geese could be seen flying over a park in the middle of town. People stopped to watch as the geese dived towards the lake and, with a rustle of wings and loud cries, skimmed the surface before settling gently on the water. Dogs barked and ducks swam to the side.

'The geese are back,' quacked one of them. 'Must be autumn.'

'Yes,' quacked another. 'The geese are back. Doesn't time fly.'

Among those in the park watching the arrival of the geese was a boy with his mother.

'Have the geese flown far?' he asked.

'All the way from the Arctic,' his mother replied.

'Why did they come to the park?'

'They come here every year and return to their homes in the spring.'

'How do they know the way?' the boy asked.

'That's their secret,' his mother replied. She looked

down and smiled. 'Shall we go home, now, Simon? You're only just out of hospital and you must be feeling tired.'

The boy nodded and his mother turned his wheelchair and pushed it away down the path.

The eldest gander and his wife hunted out a hollow in the ground and built a nest of leaves and grass. When they had finished, the gander lay down.

'I'm very tired,' he groaned.

'I'm not surprised,' said his wife. 'Terrible winds we had. I wasn't sure we were going to make it at one point. We'd have been blown right off course if it hadn't been for you. Now you stay put, my dear, and I'll find some food.'

Winter came, and in the park the geese built their nests, rested after their hard journey, swam on the lake, chatted with the ducks, and watched the people. And the people in the park watched the geese. Every day, Simon and his mother walked down the path beside the lake and looked at the nest. On most days the eldest gander would be there, lying half-asleep.

'He doesn't swim as much as the rest,' said Simon. 'And that other goose brings him food, as if he was a baby.'

'Perhaps it's taking him a long time to recover from the journey,' said his mother. 'And if *you* want to recover quickly, Simon, you should exercise.'

She helped him out of his wheelchair and, holding on to her tightly, Simon walked up and down the path.

'Perhaps he's been ill, like me,' said Simon, ' and his legs are stiff.'

But the eldest gander was not ill, although his limbs were stiff and his wings pained him when he tried to fly.

'What is it, my dear, what's wrong?' asked his wife one night as they lay curled together in their nest.

'I feel cold,' said the gander, 'and my limbs ache.'

The goose spread her wings over him. 'There,' she said, 'that'll soon warm you. Try to sleep now, my love.' And the gander closed his eyes, but he could not sleep for worrying about how he would manage the long flight home, while beside him his wife also lay awake, worrying about the same thing.

Christmas came and there was a carol concert in the park.

'What are they singing about?' asked the gander. 'I can't hear.'

The goose flew to the other side of the lake.

'They're singing about the birth of a baby called Jesus, who is king of the world,' she said on her return. 'They are singing about how Jesus looks after everyone in the world. Perhaps,' she said quietly, settling close to the gander to warm him, 'he looks after us, too.'

Winter passed, and with the first stirrings of spring, the geese began to think of returning to the Arctic. The goose thought of the tundra with longing.

'The snow will be melting now, running down into the lakes, and the air will be fresh and clean,' she thought to herself. 'Oh, I can almost smell it! How lovely it will be to get home!'

The gander's brother swam across the lake to them. 'Is it time to go?' he asked.

The eldest gander shook his head. 'Not yet,' he said, for his wings still hurt when he tried to fly.

Simon could walk now, although he needed to lean on his mother for support. Every day he came to watch the geese, and the geese, in their turn, watched him.

'Isn't he doing well!' exclaimed the goose, with motherly satisfaction. She looked at her husband. 'And you'll do well too, once we get you home,' she said, cheerfully. But in her heart she knew otherwise, and her husband knew otherwise too.

Daffodils began to poke their heads through the grass in the park, and delicate green leaves began unfurling on the branches of the trees. The geese grew restless and kept asking, 'Is it time?' But the eldest gander still shook his head.

'Aren't the geese leaving it a bit late to fly home?' asked the duck. 'I've never known them stay so long.'

The boughs of the trees dripped with blossom, the daffodils shone in a glory of gold and the mild weather brought more people into the park. Simon could walk the whole length of path beside the lake, but the eldest gander still could not fly.

'You'll be going back to school soon,' Simon's mother said, smiling to see him walking unaided.

'Yes,' said Simon. 'I'll like that.' But he looked at the gander's nest and was worried. 'I don't think he's any better, is he?'

The geese were worried too. 'Surely it must be time now?' they asked one another. They came to the nest and asked, 'How are you?'

The eldest gander looked at them sadly, and sighed.

'My friends,' he said. 'The winter has passed and I have not regained my strength. My body is old and my wings are stiff and painful. Some other goose must lead you back to the tundra, for I can no longer fly.'

The geese looked at one another in dismay. Then the gander's brother spoke.

'I'm very sorry, brother, but if we're to go—and we've already stayed longer than we should—then we must fly soon. With your permission, I'll lead the flock home.'

The goose stood at the edge of their nest,

watching the other geese make trial flights across the lake.

'You must go with them,' urged the eldest gander.

'What nonsense,' she replied. 'Of course I won't.'

'But you *must*,' her husband insisted. 'You must go home.'

For a moment, the goose was tempted. She thought of the wide open spaces of the tundra she loved. Then she looked at her husband, struggling to climb out of the nest, and made her decision.

'Do you really think I'd leave you?' she asked. 'Don't be so silly! We'll stay here together and welcome the geese back in the autumn.'

So, when the flock of geese rose from the lake in the park, formed into a 'V', turned and headed north, the goose and the eldest gander stayed behind. 'Goodbye!' the geese called, as they flew over the park. 'Goodbye!'

'Why haven't the goose and the gander gone with the rest?' asked Simon.

'I don't think he can fly,' said his mother.

'That's sad,' said Simon, 'because I can walk now. I can run too!' And he ran off down the path to prove it.

As spring slipped into summer, the eldest gander grew stiffer. He even found it difficult to walk to the lake for water.

'He's thirsty,' said Simon, who still came to watch them, although he was now back at school. The next day, he came with a plastic bowl from home.

'Here's some water for you,' he said to the gander as he filled the bowl with water from the lake. He laid it near the nest. 'I'll come every day to fill it up,' he promised.

'Well,' said the goose in surprise. 'There's a kind boy! And isn't it nice to see him running about like that!'

The sun grew stronger and the grass began to wither and dry up. The goose had to travel long distances to find food for herself and her husband, and she grew tired.

Simon was not the only person in the park who

knew about the geese. The gardeners also knew, as did the regular walkers in the park, and everyone was concerned as they saw the goose and the gander grow weaker. They began to bring fresh grass to the nest, and Simon's bowl was filled with water twice a day. The geese were grateful and began to revive.

But it was a hot summer and, as the gander could no longer fly into the shade of the trees, he suffered as the sun shone down on their nest. The goose arched her wide wings over him to give him protection.

'You mustn't do that,' said the gander. 'You'll get burnt!'

'I'm all right,' said the goose, although she could feel the sun burning her feathers.

Simon saw them hunched together as the sun beat on their nest. He told the gardeners, and they came with their hose-pipes and sprayed cool water over the birds, and one evening they brought leaves and branches and built a shelter for the nest.

'There,' Simon said to the geese, 'now you'll keep nice and cool.'

'How kind they've been,' said the goose, as she and the gander curled up that night and watched the leaves of their shelter swaying gently in the soft summer breeze.

'Yes, 'said the eldest gander, looking at her with

his eyes full of love, 'but no kinder than you.'

Summer passed, the sun lost its strength and the leaves turned gold. The gander could walk now, and even swim, but he would never again be able to fly.

Every day the goose looked anxiously up at the sky. 'Soon they'll be here,' she said to the gander.

And, on a blustery day which sent the brown leaves hurtling from the branches, there came a rustling of wings and a loud crying as the flock returned.

'How are you! We've missed you!' the geese cried, as they settled on the lake.

The goose and the gander walked down the bank and swam to meet them. 'We're very well,' they said. 'Very well indeed.'

'How they've all grown,' the goose said that night.

'Yes,' said her husband, 'and next year you must travel back home with them, for I'll be well looked after.'

But the goose just shook her head. 'My home is with you,' she said contentedly, as she curled herself close to the gander and fell fast asleep.

10

THE ANGRY SNAKE

The snake-charmer took out his flute and began to play. A crowd formed in the town square as a large black cobra rose slowly and gracefully from a basket at the man's feet and began swaying gently in time to the music. The crowd murmured and sighed with pleasure. The music stopped, the snake sank back into the basket, and the snake-charmer bowed and smiled.

He began to play once more, a lively tune, and a long, thin, green snake emerged. But, instead of rising slowly and gracefully, this snake came up with a hiss, twisted her head, spat at the snake-charmer and quickly slithered back into the basket. The crowd began to boo. A rotten tomato was thrown, then another, and the snake-charmer stuffed his flute away, picked up the basket and fled. The two snakes were jolted up and down as he ran through twisting cobbled alley-ways. Behind them, they could hear the shouts of the crowd.

'Why did you do that?' asked the cobra.

'Because he's a rotten flute player,' replied the green snake.

'Tell me something I don't know,' said the cobra breathlessly. 'But does it really matter? We've all got to earn our crust of bread—not that I eat crusts myself, having lost all my teeth—and now there'll be nothing for supper. Oops, 'scuse me, dearie!' she added, as the basket lurched and she became entangled with the green snake.

'I've got my pride,' said the green snake.

'Pride won't put food into your stomach,' said the cobra, disentangling herself with difficulty.

The two snakes went hungry that night, as the snake-charmer fled to the next town. The following day he set up in the market square and began to shout.

'Roll up, roll up, ladies and gentlemen, come and see the most amazing, the most wonderful sight in the whole of Egypt! With my magic flute I shall charm the two deadliest, most venomous snakes in the empire!'

'Who's he trying to kid?' snorted the green snake.

'Just as well the audience won't know that I haven't any fangs.' murmured the cobra. 'I'm sure the master doesn't like deceiving people, but there you go, dearie, that's show business for you, and we've all got to live.'

A large crowd gathered and the music began. The cobra rose out of the basket and twirled gracefully round the snake-charmer's head. The audience cheered.

'Give him his due,' said the cobra when she returned to the basket, 'he might be a lousy flute player, but he can pull a good crowd. And they seemed to like my new dance, didn't they?'

The tune changed. 'Go on, dearie,' urged the cobra. 'Get out there and wow them!'

But the green snake lay in the bottom of the basket and refused to budge.

'Go on!' hissed the cobra. 'Loosen up a bit. Let yourself go. He's not *that* bad a player!'

'Shan't,' said the green snake. 'He knows that particular piece of music gives me a headache. He's only doing it to annoy me, and I'm fed up with popping in and out of baskets just because he says so. It's not right and it's not dignified. From now on, he can play his flute without me!'

The music stopped abruptly and the snake-charmer's head appeared at the opening of the basket. 'Come on out, you miserable worm,' he muttered, poking a large stick inside.

'Worm is it? Huh!' said the green snake, affronted. The stick prodded her between the eyes.

'If you don't come out this instant,' the snake-charmer threatened, 'I'll slice you in two and roast you for supper!'

'Oh you will, will you…?' replied the green snake angrily, and before her master had time to straighten up, she was out of the basket and had sunk her fangs deep into his neck. The crowd gasped, the snake-charmer fell to the ground, and the cobra slithered out to see what was happening.

'Oh dearie, whatever have you done?' she asked, appalled.

The green snake looked at the still figure. 'I think… I think I've killed him,' she wailed. 'Oh, how dreadful. How awful.' And, without another word, she slithered across the market square and disappeared.

Some days later, on a lonely road many miles from town, a vulture watched the progress of a long, thin green snake with interest. From his vantage point high on a rock, the vulture saw the snake slide slowly and wearily along the road. The snake's skin was dull and lifeless and hung in folds around her thin body. The vulture flew down, licking his lips as the snake stopped, twitched for a moment, then lay still.

'What *am* I going to do?' the green snake asked, in a thin thread of a voice.

The vulture was disappointed. 'If you're asking me, I haven't a clue,' he said crossly. 'But perhaps you can answer *my* question: are you alive or dead? If you're dead, I'll eat you, but if you're still alive, I'll wait 'til you're dead before eating you, because I was well brought up. Besides,' he continued, 'you'd give me stomach-ache if I ate you alive.'

'I am alive,' said the green snake unhappily, 'but I wish I wasn't.'

'I wish you wasn't, too,' said the vulture cheerfully. 'Never mind, you look half dead to me, so perhaps it won't be long. However did you get into that state?'

'I—I killed my master, the snake-charmer,' the

green snake confessed. 'I didn't mean to, and I'm so sorry. I was angry. I just wish I could tell him how sorry I am, but it's too late.'

'I wouldn't worry about it, if I was you,' said the vulture.

'But I *do* worry about it,' the green snake replied. 'Night and day I worry about it. If only I could put the clock back! He was a terrible flute player, but he didn't deserve to die.'

The vulture was not interested. 'So, where are you heading?' he asked.

'I don't know,' cried the green snake. 'And I don't care. I wish I was dead.'

'You soon will be if you go on like that,' said the vulture, hopefully.

The green snake sighed and began to slither further along the road.

'I'll keep you company,' said the vulture. 'And then I can be in at the kill, if you see what I mean.'

'Do what you want,' said the green snake, without interest.

So the vulture and the snake travelled through the desert together, and the vulture watched eagerly as the snake grew weaker and weaker.

'Won't be long now,' he said to himself, gleefully.

On the third day of their journey, they saw a small group coming towards them. A donkey plodded along wearily, with a girl on his back. She cradled a baby in her arms. A man walked beside them, and all of them looked travel-stained and tired.

The donkey stopped when he saw the green snake.

'It's all right,' said the green snake. 'It's all right, I won't hurt you.' She sighed. 'I wouldn't hurt a flea,' she said, and burst into tears.

The baby stirred and also began to cry.

'He needs feeding,' said the girl and, while she fed the baby, the green snake told the donkey her story. When she had finished, the donkey nodded his head in understanding.

'I know all about being angry,' he said. 'For I was the worst-tempered donkey in Bethlehem until I met my master.'

The green snake looked at the man, who was preparing an evening meal.

'Oh no,' said the donkey. 'Joseph's not my master, although he's a good man. That baby's my master. He's king of the whole world and cares for everything in it.'

'Everything?' asked the green snake.

'Even me,' said the donkey, 'and if you knew what I *was* like, you wouldn't have come anywhere near me.' He grinned. 'You wouldn't have been able to, for I'd have kicked you!'

'Do you think,' the green snake said slowly, 'do

you think your master would care for me as well? Even after what I've done?'

'Oh yes,' said the donkey. 'I'm sure of it.'

The green snake looked at the baby. The baby stopped feeding, turned his head, and looked at the green snake. And all of a sudden the green snake felt as if a terrible burden had been lifted from her. She felt that she had been forgiven. Overhead, the vulture screamed angrily and flew away, for he could see that he had been cheated of his supper.

'The desert's a dangerous place,' said the green snake. 'Would you let me travel with you? I can show you the way and protect you from harm.'

'But we're going to Egypt,' said the donkey. 'And you're going the other way.'

'I'm going where you're going,' said the green snake. 'If you'll let me.'

So the green snake travelled back to Egypt with Mary, Joseph, Ezra the donkey and the baby Jesus.

'Why are you journeying through the desert?' she asked the donkey, as she slithered along beside him. 'Shouldn't the baby king be at home in his palace?'

'By rights he should,' the donkey agreed. 'Not that he's ever lived in a palace, mind, for he was born in a stable. But we had to get him out of reach of the other king. King Herod, that is. When he heard about the baby, he didn't like it one little bit. He'd have killed

him if he'd found him. Stands to reason, I suppose,'
he added thoughtfully, 'for Herod's only king of the
Jews while Jesus is king of the world.'

'Well, you'll be safe soon,' said the green snake.
'For we're almost in Egypt.'

They crossed the border and entered a town.

'Thank you for your help,' said the donkey. 'What
will you do now?'

'Me?' said the green snake. 'I don't know. But
thank you for *your* help, too,' she said, looking at the
baby, who smiled at her as the group walked away.

The green snake turned and, as she did so, she felt
the ground vibrate to the sound of a nearby flute.

Then came a voice she had heard before.

'Roll up, roll up, ladies and gentleman! Don't miss the experience of a lifetime! Watch the one and only deadly black cobra perform her celebrated dance! See her sway to the magical music of my flute!'

The green snake slithered through the fast-gathering crowd, just in time to see the cobra rise out of her basket.

'Hello dearie,' said the cobra, dipping and swaying in time to the music. 'Nice to see you.'

'I thought the master was dead,' cried the green snake. 'I thought I'd killed him!'

'You can't kill him that easily,' said the cobra. 'You're not the first snake that didn't like his playing. If you'd only waited instead of rushing off like that, you'd have seen him recover.'

'But doesn't he hate me?' asked the green snake.

'Hate you? 'Course he doesn't!' said the cobra, winding herself round the snake-charmer's neck. 'He'll be ever so glad to see you, you mark my words. Won't you dearie?' she said, pressing her face close to the snake-charmer's. The crowd gasped and the cobra laughed and moved away. 'One snake doesn't make a good act,' she said, 'even when the act's as talented as me!' She began to sink down into the basket. 'Come on—come home. We've missed you.'

But the green snake waited until the snake-charmer saw her and held out both hands to greet her. She coiled herself around his head then, with a sigh of pleasure, she slipped into the basket.

The cobra opened one eye. 'He's still a lousy flute player,' she said, 'but you can get used to anything if you try hard enough.'

11
THE CAT WHO COULD NOT PURR

When the temple cat died, all Egypt went into mourning. For the cat who lived in the temple was no ordinary alley cat. Her name was Bast and she was sacred to the goddess Bast. For many Egyptians, the temple cat *was* the goddess herself, so the cat's funeral was elaborate, expensive and very, very long.

Once it was over, the hunt was on to find Bast's successor. Wise men were consulted and the priests of the temple were sent to every corner of Egypt. After months of searching, they returned with a three-week-old kitten who, they said, was the chosen one of the goddess.

If the old cat's funeral had been elaborate, expensive and very, very long, the enthroning ceremony of the new cat—also called Bast—was even more elaborate, stupendously expensive, and went on for weeks. Hundreds of thousands of people flocked to the city of Bubastis to see the tiny kitten, who sat cowering in the middle of an enormous throne of crimson and gold silk.

After the festivities were over, it was a very tired kitten who was placed in a big, soft bed, but it was a long time before she could get to sleep. She missed her mother and the rest of her family, and knew that she would never see them again.

Bast soon got used to her new life. Her days were spent in the Throne Room, seeing pilgrims, receiving homage and answering petitions, which she did by lifting her delicate paw or shaking her tiny head. Each evening, as the Egyptian sky darkened to a deep, velvety blue and the silver crescent of the moon appeared over the edge of the temple wall, Bast was carried onto the terrace to be seen by the adoring crowds, and there was singing and dancing until late into the night.

Bast lived in luxury. She was worshipped and pampered and had an army of servants to attend to her every wish. If Bast wished to eat, the choicest foods were sent from all parts of Egypt. If Bast wished to play, there were always people to throw balls for her to run after in the beautiful temple garden. She was the envy of every cat in Egypt. As Bast grew from a kitten to a cat, she gradually forgot her mother and brothers and sisters. Life in the temple, as the goddess's sacred cat, became the only life she could remember.

But as the years passed, Bast began to feel that something was wrong. She took to rising in the middle of the night, slipping out through a small door in the wall of the temple garden to roam the streets of Bubastis.

She met the ginger tom one night in a poor part of the town. He was lying in a patch of moonlight, his back against the stone wall of a house. He was a solid, rough, no-nonsense cat, the sort who would be good in a fight. His worn and battered face wore a contented smile, and he was purring.

'What are you doing?' asked Bast.

The ginger tom opened one eye.

'Purring,' he replied. He closed his eye and began to purr again.

'How do you do it?' Bast asked, curiously.

The ginger tom opened both eyes in surprise. 'I don't know,' he said. 'I've never thought about it.'

'I can't do it,' said Bast.

'You can't?'

Bast shook her head.

'How do you know?' asked the ginger tom. 'Have you ever tried?'

'I don't have to *try* to do anything,' said Bast, drawing herself up to her full height. 'I am Bast, the goddess's sacred cat.'

The ginger tom looked at the sleek, elegant cat standing in front of him, with her small proud head, her delicate features, her slanting eyes and her beautiful coffee-and-cream-coloured coat.

'You might be Bast, but you're still a cat,' said the ginger tom. 'And all cats can purr.'

He began to purr again, and Bast tried to copy the noise he made.

'I can't do it!' she said, frustrated. 'And I want to. It sounds so nice.'

'It is nice,' said the ginger tom.

Bast returned to the temple and summoned her priests and advisers.

'I want,' said Bast, 'to purr.'

A murmur ran through the hall. 'Bast wants to purr! Bast wants to purr!'

'How,' she continued, 'do I do it?'

Her priests and advisers looked concerned and muttered among themselves.

'I believe, Your Excellency,' said her chief adviser at last, 'that cats purr if they are stroked…'

A gasp went round the throne room. It was forbidden to touch the sacred Bast, on pain of death.

'All right then,' said Bast. 'Stroke me.'

She lay down on her silken throne. Her priests and advisers looked at one another.

'Come on', said Bast. 'Stroke me! I command it!'
She closed her eyes.

Her chief adviser turned to the other priests, but
they had run away to the far end of the throne room.

'With Your Excellency's permission...' he began,
hesitantly, and began to crawl on hands and knees up
the many steps to where Bast sat on her great throne.
He reached the top, and, with a trembling hand,
leaned forward to touch Bast's fur.

Bast pursed her mouth: 'P... P...' She tried again.
'Pr... Pr...' She opened her eyes.

'Oh, you're no good,' she said impatiently. She
pushed him away with her paw and the chief adviser

fell to the bottom of the steps. After that, no one was willing to try to stroke Bast.

'Perhaps Your Excellency should see a doctor...?' suggested one of the priests.

'Perhaps I should,' said Bast. 'Send for one!'

Doctors came from all over Egypt. They arrived with big fat papyrus scrolls, cases of instruments and serious expressions. They consulted their scrolls, examined Bast, gave her pills and nasty-tasting medicine and talked gravely with one another. At last, they shook their heads. In their opinion, they said, there was no medical reason why the cat belonging to the goddess Bast, the incarnation of the goddess herself, should not purr. But how to help her was beyond their powers.

'So what am I to do?' asked Bast.

'Actors might be able to help, Your Excellency,' they said, so actors were summoned from all over Egypt to try to teach Bast to purr.

'It's all a question of flattening your tongue and vibrating it,' the actors said, and demonstrated. Soon the whole court was purring away, from the lowest kitchen maid to the chief adviser, but it was no good. Bast still could not purr.

In despair, and in order to get some peace and quiet away from her noisily purring court, Bast again slipped out of the temple.

She found the ginger tom lying in the same place as before.

'Hello,' he said. 'Any luck?'

Bast shook her head. 'No.' She sighed. 'Everyone seems to be able to purr without any trouble at all. Why can't I?'

The ginger tom shrugged. There seemed to be no answer.

'Tell me,' asked Bast, 'when do you purr?'

The ginger tom thought. 'When I'm happy,' he said at last.

'What makes you happy?' Bast asked.

'A bit of food, somewhere comfortable to sleep, a friendly hand to stroke me from time to time... nothing much, really.'

'But I have all the food I can eat,' cried Bast. 'I sleep on the softest bed of white satin cushions, and I can command people to stroke me whenever I choose. And still I can't purr.'

'Are you happy?' asked the ginger tom.

'I don't know,' said Bast, doubtfully. 'I *should* be happy. After all, I am the likeness of the goddess come to earth and I can do anything I want...' She looked at the ginger tom. 'Can you help me?'

The ginger tom scratched himself in silence for a moment.

'Well...' he said at last. 'I've heard talk about a

child who, it's said, will be the greatest healer of all.'

'I've seen healers,' said Bast. 'I've seen the finest doctors in the land.'

'Apparently this one will be different.'

'Where is he?' Bast asked eagerly. 'I'll summon him to the temple today!'

'I don't know. Where he and his family lives is anyone's guess.'

'How can I find him, then?' Bast demanded.

The ginger tom got slowly to his feet and stretched, yawning. 'If you want him badly enough, you'll find him,' he said at last, and walked off into the house.

Bast summoned her priests and advisers.

'It has been said that this child will be a great healer, so he must live in a great temple,' she said. 'Perhaps he is a god, like Re, the sun-god, or Geb, the earth god. It shouldn't be too difficult to find him.'

But it was. The child could not be found, and Bast began to despair. She stopped giving audiences in the Throne Room and sat, day after day, staring into space, trying to purr. At night, she wandered round the temple garden, unable to sleep. She lost her appetite and grew thin. Her servants, advisers and priests were worried. They tried to tempt her to eat with a succession of the fattest mice that could be found in Egypt, but she only waved them away. They brought in musicians to play her soothing music, but Bast only closed her eyes. They sent out for brightly decorated balls to amuse her, but Bast refused to chase after them.

It was late one night, when the temple garden was drenched in the silver light of the full moon, that Bast remembered the words of the ginger tom: 'If you want him badly enough, you'll find him.'

She got up, walked through the small door in the wall and went out into the city.

She walked and she walked. From city to city, from village to village, through the length and breadth of Egypt, Bast searched for the child who, it had been said, would be the greatest healer of all.

The small house lay at the very edge of the village, a long, long way from the city of Bubastis. Wood was stacked high in the courtyard and the ground was covered with a soft coating of wood-shavings. From inside the house came the sound of hammering. Lying against the courtyard wall in the late afternoon sun was a ginger tom cat. It was purring, a loud, contented purr.

Bast stopped wearily, too tired to go further that day.

'Excuse me,' she said, 'but I'm looking for...'

The cat stopped purring, stood up and walked towards the house.

'Wait a minute!' Bast called in sudden recognition. 'Wait! Aren't you…?'

But the cat had gone. Bast leaned against the wall and closed her eyes. She was no longer the sleek, pampered cat of the temple. She had not eaten for days and she was lean and half-starved, while her coat was dirty, tangled and matted. Suddenly she felt hands, small firm hands, touching her thin body. She was picked up, held tightly. She felt a warm human cheek rubbing against her coat, then a warm hand began to stroke her gently and rhythmically, up and down. For a moment, she struggled to be free.

The child spoke softly into Bast's fur. 'Don't be afraid. I'll look after you.'

Bast relaxed.

'Jesus!' called a voice. 'Come in now for your supper.'

Bast opened her eyes and saw a woman drop to her knees beside the child.

'Poor little thing, she looks half-starved,' she said. 'Bring her in with you and we'll give her food and drink.'

The child got to his feet. Cradling Bast carefully in his arms, he began to walk towards the house. He bent his head and his warm breath tickled the fur on the cat's ear.

'Love you,' the child whispered.

And Bast began to purr.

12
THE DORMICE FIND SHELTER

The dormouse and his family should have stayed asleep for another three months, but they awoke to the sound of traffic. The baby started squeaking, Mrs Dormouse complained of the noise, and the dormouse wondered what on earth had made him build a nest beside the busy main road.

They could not get to sleep again so, looking for somewhere more peaceful, they scurried across the village green, past the pub and up Church Lane. No one saw them, for everyone was indoors on that bitterly cold December afternoon. They scampered under a lych-gate and ended up in the churchyard.

'You know what you've gone and done,' Mrs Dormouse complained, once they had recovered from their journey. 'You've only left all our nuts behind. We've nothing to eat. You'll have to go back and fetch them.'

It was true. The big store of nuts they had worked so hard to stockpile for the winter was now far away in the nest by the main road, and the dormouse couldn't remember the way back.

'Oh dear,' he said. 'I am stupid.'

'Yes,' agreed his wife. 'You are.'

'At least it's quieter here,' said the dormouse, through chattering teeth.

'It might be quieter, but we'll have to find somewhere a bit warmer,' said Mrs Dormouse. 'It's freezing, and the baby's turning quite blue.'

By the time they had squeezed themselves under the door to the church, they were all turning blue with cold. But at least they had found shelter from the bitter wind.

They scurried down the church aisle, then stopped in surprise.

'It's a tree!' exclaimed Mrs Dormouse. 'All lit up! How very strange.'

'Perhaps we could make a nest at the bottom of it,' suggested the dormouse.

'Wouldn't be warm enough,' said his wife, shaking her head. 'And besides, there's nothing to make a nest with. We need twigs and grass and leaves to make a nest. Or straw. Now a bit of straw would be nice and cosy.' She looked at her husband. 'You'll just have to go outside again and find us something.'

The dormouse shivered at the thought. Reluctantly, he turned to go, and then rubbed his eyes in disbelief. For there, in front of him, piled under a brightly lit table, was straw. Piles and piles of straw.

'And just look,' said Mrs Dormouse, pointing excitedly. 'There's even a little bed for our baby.'

The dormice settled themselves comfortably,

tucking the baby mouse warmly into the empty crib.

'I hope the owner doesn't mind us using it,' said the dormouse, anxiously.

'He's not here *to* mind,' said his wife, practically. 'So stop worrying. You are a one for worrying. And we won't stay long. Just until we've got warm and had a bit of food.' She glanced at her husband. 'Have you thought about food?' she asked.

'I'll go and search for some,' the dormouse said in a resigned voice.

But before he could climb out of the nest, the church door opened. The dormice dived under the straw. They heard rustling and chattering and footsteps. People were coming. Lots of people. The dormice were frightened.

Then everything went quiet until the people started singing. The dormouse cautiously lifted his head, eyes alert, whiskers bristling for danger, ears pointing this way and that. He blinked at what he saw. There were lights everywhere, gently flickering flames glowing from hundreds of candles.

Someone began to tell a story and the dormouse snuggled back and listened. He had always liked stories. He heard about some shepherds, and a special star and a mother, father and baby who had to take shelter in a stable one cold winter's night.

'A bit like us,' the dormouse said quietly to his wife. But his wife was fast asleep and snoring gently.

The dormouse listened carefully. He heard that this newborn baby was called Jesus, and that he was a special baby, the king of the whole world. He heard that Jesus cared for the world and everything in it.

It was a wonderful story and the dormouse forgot all his worries as he listened. He even forgot how cold it was, for a warm feeling had started at the tip of his tail and spread right to the ends of his whiskers. He poked his head further out of the nest and his nose twitched.

'Perhaps,' he thought, 'this Jesus even cares for dormice, although he's probably never heard of us.'

When the story ended, the dormouse settled himself comfortably in the straw and fell fast asleep. He woke up to find the church dark, the people gone, the baby squeaking miserably and Mrs Dormouse prodding him with her paw.

'You must go and look for food,' she said. 'Otherwise we'll all die.'

The dormouse sighed, climbed out of his warm nest and began crossing the big church. Then he remembered the story. 'If it's true that Jesus does care for everything,' he thought, 'perhaps he will help me find some food.'

Suddenly he stopped, twitched his nose, turned, and stared in amazement. For there, on the floor, was a pile of crumbs, all that remained of a mince pie. The dormouse sniffed and took a cautious nibble. A delighted smile spread across his face.

After their meal the dormouse and his family took some of the straw and made a nest of their own behind an old pew. As they settled the baby, the dormouse said, 'Wasn't that story wonderful?'

'What story?' asked his wife.

'The story of Christmas. It's about a special baby called Jesus who cares for all living things. I did wonder at the time whether Jesus knew anything about us, but when I found that food I was sure that he does.'

His wife looked at him.

'I don't know what you're talking about,' she said. And when the dormouse told her the story he had heard, his wife just shook her head.

'I don't know anything about a special baby, or a star, or a stable.' Mrs Dormouse looked at her husband, fondly. 'You probably fell asleep and dreamed it. Silly old thing.'

The dormouse smiled as he settled beside his wife and baby in their straw nest. He knew better. And, just before he fell asleep, he thought how glad he was to have found out about Christmas.

TO END...

The hare burst into the field and raced round and round, jumping up and down, his long ears quivering, his short tail bouncing.

'Say you guys, c'mon out of your burrows!' he shouted. 'Have you heard the news?'

'What's he on about now?' asked a skunk, wearily.

'Have *you* heard?' the hare asked, thrusting his face into the skunk's den.

'What?' said the skunk crossly.

'About the new baby,' said the hare. 'It's so wonderful, so fantastic, I can't keep it to myself!'

And he raced once more round the field, jumping and laughing.

'What baby?' asked the skunk, coming out of his den and looking round the field.

'Don't tell me the rabbits have had *another* baby,' said a badger in a bored voice.

'That's not news—those rabbits are *always* having babies,' said a shrew disapprovingly.

'No, it's not the rabbits,' shouted the hare, 'it's the *special* baby I mean! Jesus! The king of the world!' And he leapt and danced from one end of the field to the other.

'Tell us something we don't know,' said the shrew and disappeared into the undergrowth.

'But that's not news,' said the badger. 'That happened at Christmas. In December. It's March now so it's not *new* news, it's *old* news.'

'Is it March already?' asked the hare, stopping suddenly.

'Yes,' said the badger.

'So how come I missed Christmas then?' asked the hare.

'Perhaps you were asleep,' said the skunk.

'Perhaps I was.' The hare scratched his head for a moment, then brightened up. 'But does it matter? Christmas isn't just for Christmas is it? It's for every day!'

And with that he turned a somersault and ran off down the field, jumping and shouting for joy.

Also available from Lion Publishing:

TALES FROM THE ARK
MORE TALES FROM THE ARK
THE RAINBOW'S END

Avril Rowlands

Mr Noah could not sleep. He lay in bed, listening to the wind howling round outside, and the snuffles and grunts of the animals inside, and he talked to God.

'Listen, God,' he said. 'It's not too late. You need a lion-tamer for this job, or a big game hunter, or at least a zoo keeper. I'm very grateful that you want to save me and my family, but I'm not cut out for the job.

'And I'll tell you something, God,' Mr Noah went on. 'I'm scared of spiders and we've got two on board!'

Three original and often hilarious books which tell just what *might* have happened on board Noah's Ark.